A LITERATURE
WITHOUT QUALITIES

ABOUT QUANTUM BOOKS

QUANTUM, THE UNIT OF EMITTED ENERGY. A QUANTUM BOOK IS A SHORT STUDY DISTINCTIVE FOR THE AUTHOR'S ABILITY TO OFFER A RICHNESS OF DETAIL AND INSIGHT WITHIN ABOUT ONE HUNDRED PAGES OF PRINT. SHORT ENOUGH TO BE READ IN AN EVENING AND SIGNIFICANT ENOUGH TO BE A BOOK.

Warner Berthoff

A Literature Without Qualities

AMERICAN WRITING SINCE 1945

University of California Press
Berkeley • Los Angeles • London

University of California Press
Berkeley and Los Angeles, California
University of California Press, Ltd.
London, England
© 1979 by
The Regents of the University of California
ISBN 0-520-03696-4
Library of Congress Catalog Card Number: 78-57305

1 2 3 4 5 6 7 8 9

For Leo Marx and William H. Pritchard

Contents

Acknowledgments ix

1. Introductory 1
2. A Generation in Retreat 15
3. Bearing Witness, Negotiating Survival 47
4. Old Masters: Henry Miller and Wallace Stevens 106
5. Prospects 152

Coda: A Note on the Influence of *Tropic of Cancer* 169

Notes 179

Index 195

Acknowledgments

An invitation by the Yale University Department of English and *The Yale Review* to take part in a bicentennial examination of American literary history led to a first outline version of these chapters, delivered as a lecture to an unseasonably heat-wilted audience in New Haven on Patriots' Day, April 1976. Opportunity to solidify that outline was provided initially by the generosity of Cornell University's Society for the Humanities, where I held a fellowship during 1975-1976. I wish in particular to thank the society's then director, Henry Guerlac, for his many practical courtesies during the year, and his assistants Olga Vrana, Emily Apgar, Pamela Armstrong, and Louise Noble for a multitude of good offices. The Olin and Uris Libraries at Cornell, the Widener and Lamont Libraries at Harvard University, the Mandrake and Grolier book shops in Cambridge, Massachusetts, and—not least in any respect—the Concord Public Library have furnished indispensable assistance. I am very much indebted to my editor, Marilyn Schwartz, for her determined attack on opacities in my arguments; insofar as any remain, the fault is not hers. It would be impossible to acknowledge all those with whom, since 1945, I have traded impressions of current American writing and who are my unwitting collaborators in this book; but I have particularly valued certain casual exchanges with Frank Bergon, Jonathan Bishop, Gordon Cairnie, Phoebe Ellsworth, Monroe Engel, Bettina Linn, Tom Parkinson, and Ann and Tirzah Berthoff.

Grateful acknowledgment is made to the following for permission to reprint excerpts from copyrighted material: Atheneum Publishers, for lines from "An Urban Convalescence" from *Water Street* by James Merrill, copyright © 1960, 1961, 1962 by James Merrill; City Lights Books, for lines from "America" from *Howl and Other Poems* by Allen Ginsberg, copyright © 1956, 1959 by Allen Ginsberg, and from "The Day Lady Died" from *Lunch Poems* by Frank O'Hara, copyright © 1964 by Frank O'Hara; Farrar, Straus and Giroux, Inc., for lines from "Argument" from *The Complete Poems* by Elizabeth Bishop, copyright © 1947 by Elizabeth Bishop, renewed 1974 by Elizabeth Bishop; Farrar, Straus and Giroux, Inc., and Faber and Faber Ltd., for lines from "Message" from *Love & Fame* by John Berryman, copyright © 1970 by John Berryman, and from "Epilogue" from *Day by Day* by Robert Lowell, copyright 1975, 1976, 1977 by Robert Lowell; Harper and Row Publishers, Inc., and Olwyn Hughes for lines from "Elm" and "Daddy" from *Ariel* by Sylvia Plath, copyright © 1963 by Ted Hughes; New Directions Publishing Corp., for lines from "Asphodel, That Greeny Flower" from *Pictures from Brueghel and Other Poems* by William Carlos Williams, copyright 1954 by William Carlos Wil-

Acknowledgments

liams, and from "What you should know to be a Poet" from *Regarding Wave* by Gary Snyder, copyright 1970 by Gary Snyder; W. W. Norton and Company, Inc., for lines from *Sphere* by A. R. Ammons, copyright © 1974 by A. R. Ammons; W. W. Norton and Company, Inc., and Chatto and Windus, Ltd., for lines from "Planetarium" from *Poems: Selected and New* by Adrienne Rich, copyright © 1975 by W. W. Norton and Company, Inc.; W. W. Norton and Company, Inc., and Laurence Pollinger Limited, for lines from "Voyages" from *The Complete Poems and Selected Letters and Prose of Hart Crane*, copyright 1933, © 1958, 1966 by Liveright Publishing Corporation; Princeton University Press, for lines from "Sadness and Happiness" from *Sadness and Happiness* by Robert Pinsky, copyright © 1975 by Princeton University Press; Alfred A. Knopf, Inc., for passages from *Souvenirs and Prophecies: The Young Wallace Stevens* by Holly Stevens, copyright © 1966, 1976 by Holly Stevens; Alfred A. Knopf, Inc., and Faber and Faber Ltd., for lines from *The Collected Poems of Wallace Stevens*, copyright 1954 by Wallace Stevens, and from *The Palm at the End of the Mind: Selected Poems and a Play* by Wallace Stevens, copyright © 1967, 1969, 1971 by Holly Stevens, and for passages from *Letters of Wallace Stevens*, copyright © 1966 by Holly Stevens, and from *The Necessary Angel*, copyright 1951 by Wallace Stevens. An earlier version of chapter two has appeared in *The Yale Review* (Winter 1979) and is reprinted in revised form with the kind permission of *The Yale Review*.

Those who know the two dedicatees and their diversely excellent work as critics and scholars may be surprised to find their names in tandem at the beginning of this book. But over many years I have learned to rely on both to keep me seriously alert to the proper tasks of critical scholarship, as I have learned also to pick their brains for clues and fresh solutions; and I have thought that a book which might, on balance, be acceptable to each of them would be a book very much worth trying to write. In a way I have conceived of Leo Marx and Bill Pritchard as this project's supervisory angels, one over each shoulder, and can only hope that in the main each will be tolerant of what he finds here. It would not be the first time they have accepted lodging in the same drafty house.

Concord, Massachusetts
October, 1978

1
Introductory

What I attempt in the chapters that follow is an account of the historical character of American writing since the 1940s, taking it as both product and critical reflection of the unprecedented imaginative epoch that has issued, a third of a century later, in our own stalled moment of uneasy and uncertain temporizing. This period, volatile beyond measure in its disturbances to public consciousness, is only now beginning to assume, in our understanding, a coherence and an identity of its own. But in keeping with everything else in contemporary life that seems unstable and undelivered, it has not yet yielded up a proper name for itself, let alone a clearly convertible legacy of titles and signatures. That is one good reason why any trustworthy approach to the literature of these years must remain tentative and provisional, a questioning rather than an argument in proof. How future times will remember the imaginative writing of 1945 to 1975 seems more doubtful to us now—will it keep any readership at all?—than was the corresponding case thirty years ago for literary record-keepers confidently awash in the bounty that had flooded in between, say, 1910 and 1945. Nevertheless, these latter years comprise the history that lies nearest us and that most insistently, if obscurely, marks our own anticipations; so that getting the whole span of it into our sights is inescapably a part of present efforts (as we have stomach for them) to calculate where we now stand and what lies ahead.

If this thirty-year period has in fact produced its identifying masterworks, we do not appear to know what they are or where exactly to find them. Certainly in this account it is not my purpose to deal with every work written by an American author since the 1940s for which high-sounding critical claims have been put forward. Nor am I primarily interested in drawing up some permanent list of anthology ratings. The difficulties of selection besetting the editor of *The New Oxford Book of American Verse* in 1976, as he extended his predecessor's overview beyond the 1940s, ratify, I think, this tentativeness.* My concern in any event is less with the particular versions of contemporary reality delivered up by individual authors, or with their separately publicized innovations of form, theme, or tone (where such innovations exist), than with the developing mind-set of the period as a whole toward the very enterprise of literary making. Consequently, the argument is pitched much of the time at a more abstract and synoptic level than will suit all tastes. But three decades after the climactic interval of Faulkner's sudden recognition as our greatest twentieth-century writer of fiction, the award in sequence

*Richard Ellmann edited the 1976 volume, F. O. Matthiessen the revised *Oxford Book of American Verse* of 1950.

to Eliot and Faulkner of the Nobel Prize for literature (in this prize's seventy-eight-year history, the one instance of successive awards to authors from the same country), and the return to the United States under armed guard of the most adamant of our modernist writers-in-exile, Ezra Pound, this has more and more seemed to me an argument needing to be blocked out and worth putting on record.

A brief glance will show, however, that I have not scanted individual authors and titles. At every point it has seemed reasonable to make explanatory inferences of the most inclusive and categorical kind and then attach representative instances to them, translating back and forth as proved convenient between particular examples and larger historical tendencies and significances. Such is the historical scholar's *circulus methodicus* in any case, as well as the way every freeminded reader shares in the odd covenant of literary accumulation, the actual process by which a portion of each era's writing gets selected out for commemoration and transmission to the future. Correspondingly, it has seemed reasonable, and in the nature of literature as a living enterprise, to make direct use of my own cumulative recollections of these years—as someone normally disposed to hope that the era and locale he was born into might be marked by events of exceptional interest and importance, yet increasingly required to take warier views and admit more disquieting premonitions about the march, or drift, or catastrophic landslide, of continuing circumstance.

This relative absence of disinterestedness has seemed to me, on balance, an advantage to critical inquiry. So at least it has commonly appeared within our always experimental New World republic of letters and learning. Has not American criticism of American writing regularly been most discerning, and most usable, in the discharge of partisan commitments? From the time of Emerson and Whitman to that of Norman Mailer and John Berryman (the shrewdest, most accurate critical intelligences, I would argue, of their respective eras), the criticism that has mattered most in the United States has worked to place itself in collaborative relation to the effort of our most venturesome poets, essayists, or storytellers in order first of all to secure a free space for them in literate awareness—a space perhaps to hang themselves, as might well happen, but not before having got a fair and full hearing. Our best workaday criticism—certainly that part of it, from Poe on, which has made a difference to actual literary history—has conscientiously aimed at appearing open-minded and freshly persuadable, sympathetic even to the most unmannerly new departures so long as there was a particle of genuineness about them. Yet it has also been severely and at times unrealistically exacting in its judgment of new performances, hastening to test the work of the moment by idealized standards of past excellence or else against some still finer possibility yet to come.

In either posture it has acted from its own urgent and unsparing sense of participatory obligation. A certain shared "jealousy for the national honor,"

Introductory

which Berryman took to be one of the chief motives for a serious poetry, has guided critical reflection as well.[1] This has been the American critic's way—as citizen of a historic commonwealth uniquely conscious of its origins in self-convened public deliberations and renegotiable civil compromises—of contributing to that renewal of the mythic promise of American life which for better or worse no rising American generation has yet failed to assert as central to its mission.

This distinctive American intention in literature comes down to us in a famous succession of texts and pronouncements. It speaks, heroically enough, in Emerson's call for an American genius who would establish for his time and place a "new confession"; in Melville's excited vision of young writers "not very much inferior to Shakespeare" incubating in the American backlands; in Whitman's genial prophecy of a poet "commensurate with his people," whose country "absorbs him as affectionately as he has absorbed it"—and not less heroically in the young Pound's whirlwind campaign for an "American Risorgimento," or in Henry James's early resolve (confronting "our great unendowed, unfurnished, unentertained and unentertaining continent, where we all sit sniffing, as it were, the very earth of our foundations") not to go along scraping secondhand surfaces but "to turn out something handsome from the very heart of simple human nature."[2] The same expansive intention remains the force behind Van Wyck Brooks's youthful dream of a literary brotherhood that could generate a new spirit of leadership within the nation, or Alfred Kazin's call for a prose fiction that might again risk carrying on its back the "whole weight" of our historical society; and when Mailer, fixing his ambition for the first time within a form and idiom satisfactorily his own, explains that in the privacy of his mind he has really been "running for President" all along and "will settle for nothing less than making a revolution in the consciousness of our time," we see that this intention has not lost impetus, but continues as an impersonal power source within what may at first have seemed the most wasteful of egotisms.[3] A certain intensity of predication, and self-predication, seems natural to the American voice in literary argument as it continually finds itself challenged, in a chronically unsettled cultural order, to nerve-racking readjustments of its own primary thrust of conscience and ambition.

In common practice the defect of this habit of intensity is reflective impatience and a craving for outsized and extreme conclusions. And critical description (which specializes in its own versions of speculative extravagance) commonly takes too little account of these methodological disturbances, these abridgments and distortions of the very possibility of clear argumentative resolution. Our criticism in general—as if fearful that its inquiries will be ruled unserious if final solutions cannot be inferred from them—insufficiently acknowledges that the objects presented to it for scrutiny have come into existence in very odd ways indeed, and are more partial in what they symbolize, more idiosyncratic as cultural and historical indicators, than the passion for critical system building can conveniently admit. What particularly distinguishes created works that do outlast their own historical moment seems always to elude attempts at a full systematization, either of their essential components or of their transacted functions in the consciousness of readers. Yet what is this distinguishing element likely to be but the very force that energizes those components and breathes life into those functions?

By serving their own immediate ends, works of art (and their makers and finders) do inevitably serve various grand collective interests—language, cultural or ideological revision and reintegration, collective memory, the recovery and enrichment of common feeling. But a willed fidelity to such interests does not by itself guarantee great achievement. If it did, we would have much more in the way of fully accomplished art than we actually get; and the scandal of major art, to critical schematization, is at all times its infrequency together with its creative singularity. Yet when the surprise of the genuinely original and accomplished has in time been absorbed, its "long foreground" in both tradition and self-preparation invariably discloses itself (as Emerson, from whom I borrow the phrase, understood in his extraordinary letter of welcome to the unknown author of *Leaves of Grass*). Then critical apprehension and accurate historical understanding become, as they must, a single exercise of mind.[4]

2

These are among the considerations framing what I have undertaken to do in this short book. Within its limits I offer it as three different but related things: an inventory, a recollective critique, and a diagnostic projection. As inventory it is partial and somewhat idiosyncratically selective; forgivably so, I trust, since what is under review spans nearly one-fifth of our national literary history, and that fifth part, moreover, during which the effective literary community has itself democratically expanded and loosened discipline to an unprecedented degree. As critique the book reflects my own intermittent reading and re-reading over the same span of time, in pursuit of the satisfactions that come in greeting any genuinely inventive new performance. As diagnosis and projection it serves a guarded but unabating hope that an American literature of real imaginative weight and moment will go on being produced, and it embodies an idea of what public circumstances and dispositions are most likely to contribute to that end.

This book also embodies a broad theoretical conviction concerning literary value most generally and the relation of literary power and effectiveness to the determining matrix of reciprocal human consciousness—the collective consciousness distilled from those overlapping civil, familial, and intersubjective conditions of experience that are the active scene of our engagement with life and that frame all our shared understandings. This conviction I will try to state as compactly as possible. It is simply that our natural focus of concern, therefore of valuation, in dealing with literature is not different from what it is with the acts and consequences that distinguish human conduct in general. What, in brief, is the governing custom and idiom of human life as we commonly know it, and desire to know it?—the life we share, the life we receive from others and in due course pass on, not without changes, to others. What are those powers and capacities actively at work in life that most charm and support us, or that in our most richly engaged moments we sense we can least do without? And how do the living agents who command these capacities, or fail in them, substantially coexist in the world of familiar experience? These are the matters we most naturally desire to hear about, in literature as in any other sphere of activity. How, most particularly, within our interlocking systems of collaborative-competitive existence (of which language itself is the most extended, but our established political custom and economic division of labor scarcely less so), do we respond to and impinge upon one another as centers or as vessels of energy and possibility? I would include within this question, taking account of *lyrical* and *confessional* modes of expression as well as those we call *epic* or *dramatic*, how each of us responds to the displaced yet still imaginable "other" within our own historical, psychological, linguistic selves;* for our interior life, too, as participants in the continuum of

---

*That manifold "other" which the succession of our own lives brings into being and whose incessant secret argument with us is—as Yeats famously remarked—the true locus of poetic invention.

historical experience, derives its energy structure from the lived, customary relationships by which each of us comes forward into his circumstantial being-in-the-world.

It can be demonstrated, I think, that every serious modern theory of human behavior, from revisionary Marxism to Piagetesque developmental psychology, converges on some such interpretive position. But if required to give it a school name, I would call it (perhaps anachronistically and certainly with all due modification) Durkheimian. That is, I would conceive of the basic activity of literary production more or less as Durkheim—at the outset of the modern anthropological era of human self-understanding—conceived of the activity of religion, as above all else an "eminent form and ... concentrated expression of the whole collective life."[5] A shared "idea of society," which to Durkheim was the "soul" of religious consciousness, may be called the soul of literature, too, whether or not that idea is directly enunciated in particular works; for it is what ultimately determines those "collective representations" concerning ordinary experience that organize even our most intimate feelings and that, as regards literature, (1) provide the writer the core materials for his distinctive refashionings and (2) coincidentally direct his reader's progressive response. Such an idea of society forms, so to speak, the distributive point of contact between the writer's effort of imagination and those apprehensions potential to his readers, present and to come. It is the point at which, within a cultural group, the perceptions everybody shares are stabilized and given their names, before being dispersed once again into a multitude of individual variations. Insofar as the fullest and commonest medium of imaginative relation and representation in actual human use is language, imaginative literature, working most directly through language, is thus the art in which the plenitude of reciprocal human experience, incessantly dividing and reconverging, can be most directly and abundantly re-created—and imaginatively criticized.*

*For Durkheim and his heirs, the "collective representations" are the primary cultural formulations common to everybody within a cultural group. They include myths, rituals, laws, verbal *topoi* or commonplaces, behavioral formulas, beliefs, and so forth; also, the unstated things that every birthright member of the culture knows to be the case in life. But *shared* and *common* do not, of course, mean *uniform,* nor are *collective representations* necessarily *consensual* ones and beyond argument as regards value and use. Correspondingly, the literary work that effects these imaginative reengagements will not do so merely harmonizingly. It will incorporate conflict and opposition (and enervation and redundancy) where these, too, are normative in experience, and will leave such elements as incompletely reconciled as they commonly are in the life we all know and share. Also it will not fail to meet resistance among its potential readers and, in proportion to its power, to find at any given moment its natural enemies. At the least there will be a shifting zone of indifference or distraction which even the greatest work cannot penetrate.

But may not these very imperfections, of the character of experience itself, be a further measure of literature's ministering truthfulness? "All the artist can do," Valéry said, "is to fashion *some thing* that will produce a certain effect on someone else's mind. There will never be any accurate way of comparing what has happened in the two minds; and moreover, if what has happened in the one were communicated directly to the other, all art would collapse, all the effects of art would disappear. The whole effort the author's work demands of the consumer would be

I hope the foregoing remarks will not be taken as some sort of circuitous oath of allegiance to either a social-realist or a representational-positivist ideology of literary value. It is not simply in supplying authors with familiar materials and attitudes that this plenum of collective experience and relationship exerts its influence. Its preexistence to literary consciousness is crucial in two even more fundamental respects. It is crucial, first, in determining the logic and imaginative strength of the formal conventions through which new literary creation takes place, even while plotting to overthrow these conventions or provoke critical resistance to them; in determining also the integrity and force that particular works so created can have for audiences equipped to respond to them. Secondly, this plenum (or common repertory) of relational experience is crucial in nourishing and bringing to effective issue the uncertain gift, or accident, of creativity itself, within the successions of human history. We pay too little attention to the actual subcommunities of imaginative cooperation required for the very existence of an effective literature and indispensable to the serious pleasure literature affords its readers. (We pay too little attention, equally, to the fragility of these communities' creative advantage, and to their chronic

---

impossible without the interposition, between the author and his audience, of a new and impenetrable element capable of acting upon other men's being. *A creator is one who makes others create.*" See "Reflections on Art" (1935), in *Aesthetics,* trans. Ralph Manheim, *Collected Works of Paul Valéry,* Bollingen Series XLV, vol. 13 (New York: Pantheon, 1964), pp. 142–143.

liability to cooptation or else self-exhaustion.) For it is only through the live circuits of established, seasoned relationship—not changeless but not casually supplanted either—that individual imaginations can find their way forward into the generousness of created truth, great or small; and for literature the most immediately important are relationships of free, pleasurable speech-exchange wherever these materialize and can enter into a continuous development.

When these vulnerable human privileges fail us, so the American poet Louise Bogan wrote in a late journal, it is as if some vital original capacity in our given being had been assassinated, and we live out only a reduced semblance of what our lives might have become.[6]

Our concern with the vitality of imaginative literature is thus, whether or not we state it as a principle, a concern with the vitality of society and relational culture as well. It is a concern above all for those normative conditions of work and exchange, and thus of temporal anticipation (what future can we imagine this present time as actually preparing?), through which all societies advance upon their own further existence. This concern is made more intense by our realization that even the greatest literature, as historically known to us, cannot by its own intrinsic power create and keep intact these enabling communities of cooperation. Literary making is not by itself capable of reforming, reactivating, the social community that furnishes it the odd chance of sustained life. Keeping watch on its own processes, as literature and the arts always have (and not only in the present self-consciously self-conscious era), it must watch with equal wariness the collective occasions it rises from. So for good or bad the criticism of literature cannot escape serving—in the broad, the proper, the concretely prophetic sense—a *political* as well as an aesthetic or metaphysical or psychological-sentimental interest.

On the whole it seems to me reassuring that the American writers we most value have seldom thought otherwise.

2
A Generation in Retreat

> You see, I have a feeling that the arts are in a very funny position now—that we are free to say what we want to, and somehow what we want to say is the confusion and sadness and incoherence of the human condition.
> Robert Lowell, interview with A. Alvarez (1965)

To ask what the activity of American writing has amounted to over the past third of a century is also to ask about its present situation and visible character, and to express a critical concern which, acknowledged or not, has grown progressively more disturbing to literary performance itself. Is the literature of our own day, in range, in resourcefulness, in effective grasp and purpose, as different in fact from the achievement we value in earlier periods, as diminished and attenuated, as increasingly many have felt it to be? And if so, by what reactive impulses and contractions—since, say, the early 1940s, the still classic moment of *Four Quartets, The Hamlet* and *Go Down Moses, For Whom the Bell Tolls, Native Son* and *Black Boy, Notes Toward a Supreme Fiction, The Iceman Cometh*—and with what comparable, Nobel-competitive monuments and milestones, if any, has it reached this present situation and acquired this felt character?

The impression of some fundamental qualitative difference does not seem to me mere backward-looking prejudice. Suppose we had raised the same sort of question half a century ago, and had taken for evidence the new books of 1925, 1926, and 1927. Admittedly not every observer would have been equally ecstatic, or ecstatic for the same reasons; yet would it not have been generally agreed that the "American Risorgimento" Pound, Brooks, and the rest had been calling for was now in a fair way to getting accomplished? Quite apart from new work by recognized writers beginning to overreach their best creative openings (*Arrowsmith, Dark Laughter, A Mother's Recompense*), a critic-historian of the moment could have mustered the following as material for judgment—and for celebration: *An American Tragedy, Manhattan Transfer, The Making of Americans* and *Composition as Explanation, The Professor's House, Barren Ground, The Time of Man, In Our Time, The Sun Also Rises* and *Men Without Women, The Great Gatsby* and *All the Sad Young Men, The Great God Brown, Soldier's Pay* and *Mosquitoes, The Hollow Men* and *Sweeney Agonistes, A Draft of XVI Cantos*, four new E. E. Cummings titles, *White Buildings, Blue Voyage, In the American Grain* (not to overlook *Porgy, Craig's Wife*, and *The Second Man, Gentlemen Prefer Blondes* and *archy and mehitabel*); and all these while alert readers were still absorbing the fresh lessons of *Homage to John Dryden, Port of New York*, and *How to Write Short Stories*, and tuning their ears to the new music of *Spring and All, Harmonium, Observations, Tamar and Other Poems, Cane, The*

A Generation in Retreat

Enormous Room, A Story-Teller's Story, from 1922 to 1924.

What comparable litany for the middle 1970s? In drawing up a representative list of new titles, my intention is not at all to borrow critical security from an earlier era's certified magnificence and dismiss the risked enterprise of a whole new generation; nor is it to lay out prima facie proof of some absolute decline and fall. The years just past have in fact supplied any willing reader with more than enough to stay cheerfully occupied. Through 1975, 1976, and 1977 our writers, seemingly undiscouraged, have given us a reassuring assortment of commodities we would be much the poorer without:

(1) expert prose entertainments, like *Humboldt's Gift* (Bellow), *1876* and *Matters of Fact and Fiction* (Vidal), *Ragtime* (Doctorow), *A Month of Sundays* and *Picked-up Pieces* (Updike), *October Light* (Gardner), *Who Is Teddy Villanova?* (Thomas Berger), *The Family Arsenal* and *The Great Railway Bazaar* (Paul Theroux), *The Professor of Desire* and *Reading Myself and Others* (Roth), *Details of a Sunset and Other Stories* (Nabokov);

(2) fictions, memoirs, miscellaneous depositions, collections of testamentary poetry, which read as homeopathic antidotes to contemporary disorders and apprehensions, such as *The Assassins* and *Crossing the Border* (Oates), *JR* (Gaddis), *Travesty* (Hawkes), *Falconer* (Cheever), *Dog Soldiers* (Robert Stone), *Zone of the Interior* (Clancy Segal), *Three Journeys* (Zweig), *Speedboat* (Adler),

The Woman Warrior (Kingston), *Of Woman Born* (Rich);

(3) patient continuations of a stubbornly developed expressive integrity which is the more admirable for everything in contemporary life that conspires against it, as in *Geography III* (Bishop), *Divine Comedies* (Merrill), *Self-Portrait in a Convex Mirror* (Ashbery), *What Thou Lovest Well Remains American* (Richard Hugo), *To a Blossoming Pear Tree* (James Wright), *Beyond the Bedroom Wall* (Woiwode), *The Widow's Children* (Fox), *Flight to Canada* (Reed), *Lancelot* (Percy), *Day by Day* (Lowell);

(4) no perceptible shortage of resolute performative novelties, like *Amateurs* and *The Dead Father* (Barthelme), "Essay on Psychiatrists" (Pinsky), *On Being Blue* (Gass), *98.6* (Sukenick), *Gala* (Paul West), *Even Cowgirls Get the Blues* (Tom Robbins), *The Public Burning* (Coover), *Why I Don't Write Like Franz Kafka* (William S. Wilson).

As to mere numbers one could easily compile a considerably longer list of writers and performances worth having it out with. But where among them all is the book or voice that convinces us it has mastered its elected materials and is not fundamentally at their mercy? Where is the one clearly empowered to change our minds (if not, as we might unreasonably wish, our lives and fortunes) or at the least to enact literature's signal function of furnishing, in Auden's moving line, "an altering speech for altering things"? Where is that work of specifically literary intelligence which by common agreement is "consistent, engaging, and dramatic, in exceptional degrees; which exhibits largely mastered a human subject of the first importance; and which seems in retrospect to illuminate the whole physical and spiritual situation of which it was, by the strange parturition of art, an accidental product"?—John Berryman's vernacular definition of what (short of "wild rivalries with Hawthorne or Stendhal") we might mean by the word *masterpiece*.[1] What new book has done so much as furnish a proper name, like "Babbitt" or "Waste Land," for the unnerving alterations of outlook, judgment, morale, which at an ever-quicker pace seem to force themselves on us beyond reversion?

No doubt comparisons of this sort are not only odious but chronologically arbitrary, being subject in the first place to quite short-term variances. Thus, the years 1928 and 1929 might not yield so extraordinary a canvass as 1925–1926; and 1967–1968 (with climaxing works by Berryman, Mailer, and Lowell for starters) would for many readers considerably shift the balance. But the commonplace point at issue would not, I think, be different: that the literary enterprise itself has changed, and in fundamental ways, since the American modernists finished their work, and that certain traditional conceptions of the goal of literary workmanship—and of the authority and value of perfected achievement—have fairly completely disintegrated.

Of course it is not only in American writing that all this has come about. A critical accounting of

British or of Continental literature in the years since the Second World War would produce much the same damping impression. Cyril Connolly's once-notorious remark, that no literary task is of any consequence except the production of "a masterpiece,"[2] reads now as a last quixotic expression of the central modernist faith (already splintering when he reaffirmed it in 1945) that significant art lives by a perfection of interior design and compels later ages to defer to it on its own unreducible terms. Surely no one now expects that British literary history between 1945 and 1975 will attract the same retrospective attention being paid to the era of Yeats and Joyce, Lawrence and Forster, Woolf and Auden; while for Europe what may chiefly want explaining is why so many of the strongest new talents of c. 1960, like the novelists Günter Grass and Michel Butor, would effectively abandon the creative mode they matured in.*

*Perhaps the significant exception—leaving aside the chronology-canceling circumstances in which Soviet-bloc authors are condemned to work—would be Latin American writing, where, particularly in the novel, an odd amalgam of incantatory realism and modernist deconstruction has greenly flourished over the past two decades: Garcia Marquez, Cortazar, Fuentes, Vargas Llosa, among others. Yet in ways that seem essential to the very profusion which makes it currently so remarkable, Latin American literature remains a colonial literature—"a literature without criticism," in Octavio Paz's telling phrase (*Times Literary Supplement*, 6 August 1976, pp. 979–980)—expressing through every surrealist refraction the awareness that real power and real responsibility are always in the hands of others. As a test of the effect of prolonged political impotence on creative consciousness, this remarkable body of work does not seem to me likely in the long run to give much comfort.

In any event one is not required to argue that, in relation either to other literatures or, for that matter, to our own national past, the genetic pool of talent and ambition in the United States has mysteriously gone dry. Quite the opposite, in fact. If we can identify any new writers worth attentive reading, and re-reading, over the past thirty or forty years, we can identify all too many; too many, that is, for purposes of a concise summing up. The selection of names in Richard Howard's accounting, in 1969, of the American poets who had "come into a characteristic and . . . consequential identity since the Korean War" is now seriously out of date and needs, if anything, expansion.[3] As it is, Howard's by no means undiscriminating book surveyed the work of no fewer than forty-one individually accomplished poets; and nearly every knowledgeable reviewer had his checklist of regrettable omissions. Further, it can well be argued that any account of this period which defined its essential character through a smaller, more exacting selection of names and titles would be historically false. It would be false most especially to our actual experience of the years in question *as* a historical period, with its own distinguishing conditions for new work and for the reception of new work; false as well to the sense that these conditions have settled over us by fits and starts and at a hundred different facings, rather than through the exemplary power of a few acknowledged master texts.

2

The odd title I have given this study as a whole proposes a way of defining what I take to be peculiar both to the present situation in our literature and to the cumulative retrenchments of recent decades. I borrow it from the title of Robert Musil's long novel of 1930–1942 (a work which, as it aimed to apply the extraordinary freedom and self-assurance of modernist writing not only to constructing another individual masterpiece but to forging nothing less than a prophecy of the world's evolutionary future and humankind's perilous way through it, was more or less predictably left unfinished; perhaps also predictably, it has been the last modernist classic to begin to be acknowledged and assimilated by official criticism). The lack of qualities of Musil's "Man Without Qualities" is of course a relative thing; so, too, is the retreat from "qualities" by which I would characterize recent literary history. Musil's hero has in fact a full complement of familiar human attributes, which he displays in attractively high resolution. He is male and in the prime of his first reflective maturity, being another of those twentieth-century heroes just turning thirty whom Theodore Ziolkowski has identified as normative in modern fiction.[4] He has wit, appetite, impatience, vanity, a certain technical and scientific expertness but a deep distrust of it as an end in itself, a touch of cruelty, a reserve of self-mockery, and so forth. He has, in short, all the attributes by which we recognize the historical species and type which, like us, he springs from.

His being defined as "without qualities" is rather a matter of a new attitude toward those accredited competences that are open to him to specialize in and profit from personally (in the manner of his antitype in Musil's scheme, the businessman-diplomat-polyhistor-saloniste Arnheim, possessor of "qualities" innumerable), competences which assign him speculative value in the eyes and expectations of others. This new attitude begins to be acted out in the permanent vacation from ordinary institutionalized life Musil's hero, together with his sister and Platonic double, voluntarily enters upon midway through the novel. He gives up the gratification of qualities for the sake of a deliberate blankness and openness before a historical ordering of life that he senses as somehow implicit in the self-forming, self-extending nature of things; a new and (as he is tempted to say) millennial conformation of experience which, more strongly than any other motive, draws him to serve it and to bear it anticipatory witness. In obscure ways the compulsion to follow this nameless new calling seems to him a first step not only toward the recovery of some lost integrity of selfhood—hence Musil's appropriation of the Platonic myth of the soul's division and self-recovery, and his attraction to the theme of incest—but toward a new evolutionary-historical state of general human existence.

We may recognize in Musil's basic story a reenactment of certain fundamental processes of developmental interruption and change which have been variously described in modern thought, from William James's tabulation of the psychic experience of the "twice-born" to Arnold Toynbee's seductive conception of great cycles of withdrawal and return in the life history of both heroes and civilizations. Behind them all, in our not yet fully de-Christianized consciousness of the discipline of being, stands, historically and typologically, the Scripturally defined experience of conversion, or self-conversion—though in a form now (to our eyes) quite unsupported by consecrating authority. The process recapitulates that personal abandonment or emptying out of distinguishing qualities and privileges which in religious language we know as *kenosis,* according to St. Paul's description in Philippians 2:7 (ἐκένωσεν) of the extraordinary act of change Christ took upon himself in entering the historical world, demystifying himself, as one might say, in order to recover control of the expansions of human consciousness.* And in finding this older term appropriate we again acknowledge, as we must, the degree to which the formulations and paradigms of religious experience—or the recollection of them and of their peculiar authority—have regularly shadowed literary history; have set their mark on the various competing agenda pursued by the classes of persons, writers *and* readers, who have been responsible for western literature's major continuances.[5]

In American writing this convergence of secular literary ambition upon essentially religious impera-

---

*Contemporary identity theory gives us the complementary psychologist's term *moratorium*; but this misses the element, beyond our simply suspending routine obligations and their drain on permanent psychic resources, of clearing them out once and for all.

tives runs very deep. More than any continuity in literary performance as such, it is what has connected one historical epoch in American writing to the next, in progressions that nearly always take on the publicized form of a compulsive emptying out, or clean sweep, of the performative stockroom. What we have had, periodically, are not simply generational progressions, with new incumbencies for fixed literary offices, but a fracturing of what currently has been understood as appropriate to literature itself; a rejection of the very notion of orthodox literary making as an acceptable enterprise, with qualities and values peculiar to itself that are worth maintaining and renewing.

The coercive model for these transformations can be described in various ways. It is, in one central respect, a *pastoral* model—and by this I do not mean the special set of poetic and mythological conventions descending in western literature from Theocritus and the Virgilian eclogues, but the ministerial pastoralism of the reformed, regathered Protestant churches (churches or priesthoods of the single believer, if necessary). Here the ruling principle is simply that effective speech, and by extension good writing, can never be an end in itself. Rather it must always be subordinate to the practical occasion that has called it forth. It should aim at becoming transparent if not strictly invisible in fulfilling its distinctive purposes—which are not (for the writer) beauty, fame, worldly honor and power, but creaturely survival, for an elect communion of oneself and certain others. In another perspective this operative model finds expression in the civil ethos of *populism,* denying any assertion of received authority, literary or otherwise, which presents itself as intrinsically superior to everyday democratic striving. (Here, too, in American fiction as also in Russian, the application regularly takes on sectarian coloring; the "people" with whom the writer and his special audience are to align themselves will be conceived as a secularized version of the New Testament's "people of God.") In yet another perspective what is acted out is a deliberate withdrawal or abdication from all *extended* responsibility or responsibility-at-a-distance, approaching at the extreme some root-and-branch privatization of living experience, or else that ascension of historical understanding into a visionary heaven of triumphant selfhood that Sacvan Bercovitch, in a formidably argued book on the Puritan origins of the American self, has identified as the self-renewing theme of nearly every subsequent American classic.[6]

To apply this broad model to the matter in hand: my conjecture here is simply that when the full history of recent American literature is written, the pivotal episodes will not be the appearance of a new set of masterworks in the old sense, latter-day equivalents of *Ulysses,* "Prufrock," *The Sound and the Fury,* and the like (whose very titles and main constitutive images call attention to their continuity with classic precedents). Rather they will be a series of moments in which certain conventionally ambitious writers decided to stop trying to do the sort of job that as writers they had set out to do, or been authoritatively taught to do, and began working in a different manner altogether, according to a different conception of value and accomplishment. And it will be seen that in first reaction to this decisive face-about, critical partisans and antagonists alike have felt compelled to raise the question of whether the texts that result really belong to the category *literature* as commonly understood.

The change in question has not of course been absolute, the abrupt displacement of an existing structure of practice and expectation by one totally different and opposed.* It appears rather as a Doppler shift along that structure's visible spectrum, to the point eventually of requiring measuring instruments with qualitatively different tolerances. It is a change that comes in at first by side doors and back alleys within basically familiar precincts; indeed many of its chief bearers will have begun their visible progress by aligning their work respectfully enough alongside the conspicuous prizewinners of the era just past or passing, and by claiming acceptance as the true inheritors and renewers of that era's mantle of achievement. Even those who aimed, after 1945, to say something radically original attached themselves so far as possible to workshop motives and purposes dating back to 1900 and 1912. (For what could be more original than late modernism's presumptuous "revolution of the word" as described in the Paris journal *transition* and elsewhere around the

---

*We recognize such myths of radical displacement as central to modernism in general, in the manner of Harold Rosenberg's "tradition of the new."

end of the twenties? Who could take more direct fictional aim than Dreiser and Hemingway had already done on the altered sense of life shared by the victims of modern city existence and the survivors of modern war?) One way, indeed, of establishing the character of the collective literary-historical event I am defining here is to remind ourselves how much there was in the literary situation of 1945 to obscure even the possibility of its occurring.

Thus if we were examining only the decade from 1945 to 1955, it would be easy to show an essential continuity of American literary ambition and practice into the second half of this century. Young writers themselves, seeking positions of advantage to start out from, explicitly assumed this continuity. Norman Mailer would not be at all untypical, systematically taking the correct steps—studying Joseph Warren Beach's *American Fiction: 1920–1940* like an operator's manual; calculating which hemisphere of combat would be likely to produce World War II's *A Farewell to Arms*—to become the Hemingway of the rising generation, rather as Hemingway himself was still belligerently inviting comparisons with various nineteenth-century heavyweights of fiction. The same efficient conservatism, we see, directs the work of Richard Wright and Ralph Ellison, separately reaching out to the powerful modern precedent of Dostoevsky's underground man as well as to the extravagances of naturalist fiction in general to give form to their vehement re-creations of black life in contemporary Chicago and New York.

Or, still arguing for a basic continuity, we might

review the career charts of that whole company of apprentice poets who in the late 1930s and the 1940s put themselves to school with one or another recognized master of the preceding generation. It is a case worth considering in some detail. These were the poets, most of them college bred, who began by seeking out the approval of teachers and editors known to take their evaluative cues from T. S. Eliot; who traveled to Kenyon College to study with John Crowe Ransom (who in turn overwhelmed them not with magisterial authority but with courtliness and good taste, qualities of mind possibly fatal to aspire to in a writer's first youth); who went on to Nashville and Baton Rouge to camp within reach of Allen Tate and Robert Penn Warren, or to Bread Loaf to breathe in the sly, untransferable self-promotions of Robert Frost, or to San Francisco and environs where they could choose between Yvor Winters and Kenneth Rexroth as mentors (and choose well in either case), or else to Paris cafés where Picasso had doodled and Hemingway watched and listened; who prowled the Grolier Book Shop, Newbegin's, Shakespeare & Company, the Gotham Book Mart, for autographs and fresh clues; who paid ritual calls on Dr. Williams in Rutherford, Marianne Moore in Brooklyn Heights, Louise Bogan at *The New Yorker,* Henry Miller at Big Sur, Pound in the fortress of St. Elizabeth's; who eagerly, helplessly (at first) absorbed and imitated the cadenced grandeur of Yeats, the conversational crispness of Auden and MacNeice, the glitter and aloof precision of Stevens—young poets, that is, whose own first breakthroughs into poetic seriousness came about as (in Berryman's precise characterization of Lowell's *Lord Weary's Castle* in 1946) "the natural product of an elaborate, scrupulous and respected literary criticism."[7]

But it would be, if we followed it to the end, a melancholy story for the most part. This gifted and superbly taught younger generation of the forties and fifties is surely our American "tragic generation" and not only in the shocking casualties it has taken, its palpable struggle with its own will to self-destruction: Weldon Kees, Theodore Roethke, Delmore Schwartz, Randall Jarrell, Charles Olson, John Berryman, Jean Garrigue, Robert Lowell, down through late joiners, father-haunted, like Anne Sexton and Sylvia Plath. There is the stuff of private tragedy also in the sense we have of its never quite emerging (or, with the two or three most fully original, emerging only by a desperate wager of selfhood against unbearable tensions and discords) from the towering shadow of its extraordinary predecessors—who, as it happened, simply refused during these same years to get out of the way.

For it is certainly possible to contend that the overshadowing events in American poetry during the ten or fifteen years after the Second World War involved not the formation of a new school and commanding new poetic but the completion of the life work of the writers of 1912 and just after—Williams, Stevens, Eliot, Frost, Pound, Moore, Cummings—as marked, historically, not only by the skillful repetitions of various followers and imitators but by the monument-completing publication, one after another, of their own last and then collected poems, and letters and essays; all in spectacular disregard of the standard American thesis that something disastrous happens to our writers at a certain age, that their brilliantly emergent careers are allowed no second acts. Rooted, temporally, in that long collaborative resurgence of disciplined freedom and originality which for lack of a better name we continue to identify as modernist, these poets turned even the final weakening of their own realized power into superbly measured verse. Even now we can ask whether since the end of the 1940s we have had any more beautiful and accomplished poems than those in Williams's *The Desert Music* (1954) and *Journey to Love* (1955) or in Stevens's *The Auroras of Autumn* and "The Rock" (1950). Can we point to anything in the famous confessional mode that can stand with Cantos 81–82 and 116–117, or recall a more securely phrased and cadenced lyric than Cummings's "now does our world descend," printed in *The New Yorker* a few months after the poet's death in 1962?

3

So described, the kind of crisis of development and change being examined in this chapter will be familiar enough to us in its broad outlines. Interestingly, it would appear to fit certain cogent models of general literary and poetic history recently elaborated for us by academic criticism, according to which younger writers more or less inevitably labor under the crippling burden of the great creative past and must struggle with only partial hope of success to break free of the terrific influence of their most admired precursors, in order to become creators of equal strength *and in the same performative mode.*[8] But the pivotal moments of change I have in mind after 1945 are really of another kind. They are moments instead when that ruling mode itself, and the conceptions of vocation and performance it presupposes, lose credit and are seemingly abandoned; and the writer begins to write, not to achieve the same kind and degree of mastery he has been schooled to admire, but simply to maintain himself as a functioning being in whatever intentional sphere he can tolerate belonging to. He writes, as it were, to reenfranchise himself; to safeguard whatever fiction of personal agency he can imagine living by from day to day. He gropes for a mode of expression which will confirm, to himself first of all, his own consequential presence in the world.

To give examples, already on record. They would be such moments as the Canadian writer Mordecai Richler has evoked in a good-humored memoir about second-generation G.I. Bill expatriates in Paris in the early 1950s when, after struggling all day with their Thomas Wolfe or James T. Farrell novels of adolescent life in various benighted and fast-vanishing American neighborhoods, they came together in the cafés to recover their spirits with ex-graduate-student parodies, nostalgic burlesques of old radio and movie scripts, or passages from the pornographic texts they were concurrently writing, under pseudonyms, to make money—until some of them had the wit to realize that these diversions were not only more entertaining as performances, and certainly more marketable, but somehow more authentically accomplished. So it was in the later fifties that a politically progressive realism or naturalism, descending from the turn of the century with only superficial changes in outlook, finally gave way as the staple of our prose fiction, and the sub-satirical *humour noir* of books like *Candy* (1955; 1964) and *The Magic Christian* (1960) was born.[9] There are New York versions of the same performative turnaround, as between John E. Kerouac's *The Town and the City* (1950) and Jack Kerouac's *On the Road* (1957); between Frank O'Hara's studious imitations of the surrealism of Apollinaire and Reverdy and those improvised lunch-hour collages in which he decided first of all to be seen, and heard, having as good a time writing poems as Larry Rivers and Grace Hartigan were having painting; or between Allen Ginsberg's self-described beginnings as "a fair-haired boy in academic Columbia" and his consciously antithetical conviction—of which *Howl* (1956) was the first poetic monument—that "a leap to living sanctity is not impossible," and that the business of his life was to be a new "*liberation* of basic human virtues."[10]

Or such a moment, around 1957, as Lowell later described, when he found himself on the West Coast giving public readings of poems that had been in print for three or four or ten and fifteen years but no longer writing very much; and a consequent concern at his own dryness moderated an instinctive contempt for the outpourings of the San Francisco crowd as he saw them in action. The San Franciscans (several of them, too, like Ginsberg, in flight from graduate schools east and west) had largely stopped writing what anyone trained at Kenyon or Amherst or Columbia would have called a poem. Nevertheless, they were writing, speaking, entertaining each other and friends. Also they were somehow staying alive as writers and as persons and having a visibly enlivening effect on actual audiences—no negligible achievement, Lowell thought, though conceding nothing to the makeshift techniques being practiced, and began writing the poems published in Part Four of *Life Studies* (1959); poems, incidentally, which take on affective life by setting out in blunt detail the story and anatomy of his own personal and poetic incapacity.[11]

Lowell's turn inward, from aggressive impersonality to a verse that discovers both matter and form in the contours of private recollection, can be matched in the careers of more than one of his university-domiciled contemporaries.[12] The idiosyncratic voicing of Berryman's *Dream Songs,* the first long set of which appeared in 1963, traces back through *Homage to Mistress Bradstreet* in 1956 to a sonnet sequence written at the end of the 1940s out of excruciating personal trouble, though not itself published—it became *Berryman's Sonnets*—until 1966. So, too, Randall Jarrell's narrower gift missed finding a form or outlet wholly congenial until the touchingly private poems of *The Lost World* (1965). Not unexpectedly, James Wright, ten years younger than his Kenyon predecessors, would make the shift from *Kenyon-Sewanee* formalism to free verse and the personal testament roughly ten years sooner in the sequence of his work. For W. D. Snodgrass (whose *Heart's Needle* appeared in 1959 and to whom Lowell has given chronological priority in these developments) the solution came by fitting a confessional impulse he had no other apparent defense against into a syncopated version of stanzaic formalism itself. But for Delmore Schwartz, the first of the older group to come to maturity as a poet, the same turn inward and corresponding relaxation of prosodic and argumentative strictness—in the longline rhapsodies of *Summer Knowledge* (1959)—seem desperate gambles in a venture of selfhood already compromised beyond recovery.*

*Yet it should not be overlooked that a corresponding transposition into the personal and confessional characterizes much of the masterly late poetry of Yeats, Eliot, Williams, and Stevens. For them, however, there is not really the same fundamental change of strategies. In *Four Quartets,* for example, the impression of a greater (or slacker) prosiness of style has to do largely with the substitution through much of the text of a single ruminative voice for the dramatistic soliloquies and choruses of earlier poems; while the five-part organization of each quartet, with the opening of the second and the whole of the short fourth section given over to a contrasting lyric formality, reproduces rather closely the organization that emerged from Pound's and from Eliot's own revisions of the "Waste Land" manuscripts. With all of these poets, Pound included, old age itself became a last concentrating subject and focus, from which certain lifelong themes ray out with a more poignant intensity.

Again, the changes being described, the widespread abandonment of the stricter disciplines of modernism, have not been absolute. Most frequently the new work proceeds by an extrapolation of one or another secondary gesture formalized during that earlier epoch. But what for the twenties writers had been self-diversifying ironies tend to emerge now as articles of single belief. A much circulated talisman from Marianne Moore's "Poetry"—"I too dislike it"—begins to be acted on quite literally, as an axiom not requiring dialectical modification; and a new generation starts trying to express with unimpeded directness, as if for the first time, those things in experience which at each instant are simply more important than all this anthology-aspiring "fiddle." If in the process these writers seemed to turn the writing of poems into some sort of "mug's game," insisting with Frank O'Hara that "the silliest idea actually in [one's own] head was better than the most profound idea actually in somebody else's head,"[13] that was no more than what Mr. Eliot himself, in *his* heyday, had grinningly conceded. (Historians will in due course take note of O'Hara's, and John Ashbery's, participation in the early 1950s in theater groups which revived, among other twenties experiments, *Sweeney Agonistes*.) Or was it Gertrude Stein who had best anticipated this rejection of perfected literary structures, her own included, as in any way superior to the preparations they develop from, in explaining why she had left unfinished *The Making of Americans* once she was satisfied that the trial of form it represented was demonstrably succeeding: "After all I know I really do know that it can be done and if it can be done why do it ..."?[14]

Nor, to repeat, is the whole idea of some terminal or else metamorphic crisis in the history of literature and the arts peculiar to the special disaffections of the last two or three decades. The meteoric career of Rimbaud's self-consuming genius and Nietzsche's sardonic prophecies and subsequent madness, in particular, burned this idea into twentieth-century consciousness, but the scandal of it was fully advertised in Hegel's lectures on aesthetics in the 1820s,[15] and, earlier still, in the conventionalized pessimism of the progress-of-poetry poem: Collins, Gray, Blake, and Wordsworth most memorably (in English). It underlies the compulsion toward silence that we identify with *symbolisme* and with the Mallarmé whom Lowell came to admire for having invented "a style that made writing impossible";[16] it is continued in Beckett's rigorous pursuit of LESSNESS, or of a final imaginative leap so violently undertaken that it accomplishes its own extinction (*Imagination Dead! Imagine*). Such minimalism, as it forces itself on American writing in the embattled 1960s, has important native precedents as well. Both the stripped yet repetitive observation poetry of James Wright and Robert Bly and the anodyne primer-prose of Vonnegut, Brautigan, and Barthelme trace directly back in recent history to Hemingway's mannerist simplifications and Williams's "no ideas but in things" (with a nearer precedent in the strangled narrative style of Delmore Schwartz's story collection of 1948, *The World Is a Wedding*); more distantly, to Poe's journalism-based notions of a frictionless expressive purity; perhaps ultimately, in American usage, to the formalized plain speaking of rigorous antinomian purifiers like the early Quakers and Baptists. For all these diverse practitioners, a fluent or genial expressiveness is potentially defiling.

But in one primary respect much of the newer American writing has broken sharply with these native traditions of stylistic self-effacement, and that is in its unembarrassed volubility—or its garrulousness, to use Helen Vendler's harsher word; its indulgence in mere self-extending talk, even at times in a kind of performative glossolalia in which absurdities of language are encouraged to argue with themselves (as in the gag-writer's dialogue which fills out much of Joseph Heller's overdrawn *Catch-22*); its spinning out of passages and chapters that appear to stop for no other reason than that the time allotted has run out or some outside interruption occurs.* A textual abundance that no longer appears concerned with formal fitness has become something like an architectonic norm. We find it encroaching upon Berryman's last volumes and the Lowell of much of *History*, as well as, more regularly, the

---

*Poets like George Oppen and Robert Creeley present an odd combination of these extremes, the expressively minimal and the garrulousness of a verse incessantly "projective," that is, without closure or concentration. Much of what they print on the page almost perfectly resists sequential reading. Yet a public recitation by the poet himself (I have heard Creeley several times, though not Oppen) can take on its own situational eloquence.

work of a James Dickey or Diane Wakoski (and upon the prose of Bellow and Pynchon as well as Heller and William Gaddis). For the Beat writers, expectably, it would be sealed as a sacred principle: combatively championed by Ginsberg as "native wordslinging"; analytically explained by Kerouac as a blowing out, jazz fashion, of sentences and paragraphs that end only as you happen to run out of breath.[17]

And it is an abundance and volubility which seem to license a lapse of interest in good *writing* in the traditional sense—an interest that by contrast Beckett stubbornly clings to—and an indifference to the qualities demanded of an art meant to be in some fashion independent of its producer's sanctioning presence. On any given day an anxious contemporary, hungry (in a line of David Slavitt's) "for company, for comfort, vital signs," may mistake such volubility for genuine energy and strength. But that mistake is simply one of the prime consequences of our epidemic yearning, against all privation and disappointment, for restitution and some palpable consequence of our own; for some cumulatively honorable place, despite the life we feel ourselves held down to, in the memorials of future times.

Our twenties writers, for all their period confidence, were familiar enough with this species of yearning. But for them it served as a major imaginative subject (as in *Gatsby* and *An American Tragedy*), to be dramatically explored and mined for its rich material ironies. Now it is exempted from all such compositional testing and appears to float free as a process-sanctifying value and principle. The yearning itself is taken as legitimizing the writing it results in.

4

Public and historical explanations of these all-but-universal transformations of attitude and purpose—this grasping for reassurance; this contraction into volubility, if the oxymoron makes sense—are not hard to find. At first one could speak as if such changes mainly had to do with the unprecedented shock of the extermination camps and of atomic warfare, symbolically entering world consciousness in 1945 ("News that brought into play our deepest fears," as James Merrill would remember that moment thirty years later in "The Book of Ephraim"). And the monstrous power over life and death thus shown to be routinely available, on a world scale, to the *revanchisme* of technology-age governments did perhaps put an end to lingering hopes that art—or anything besides unwarranted political luck—could rescue the civilized world from an eternity of self-mutilation.

But fear of military holocaust has been only the concentrated form of a more pervasive apprehensiveness. ("What people really fear," Walker Percy's quality-shedding "moviegoer" remarks on *his* thirtieth birthday, "is not that the bomb will fall but that the bomb will not fall....")[18] Much of this has come in response to the seemingly irreversible expansion of the coercive power accruing to governments, economic bureaucracies, thought-control agencies, in an advanced technological society: the target of Norman Mailer's Carlylean denunciations of "totalitarianism," "technologyland," or (interiorized in a sullen popular inertia) "the wad." Yet even if there were saints at every control point, the sensible condition of things would not be different. We would still feel ourselves adrift without preparation in the whole new globe-spanning system of unrestricted, undelayed communication and signal-transmission; a system that not only overloads the receiving consciousness but conspires to reduce it to the status of a tributary relay. Under the assault, mind loses confidence in its simplest readings of temporal succession, its everyday grasp of possibility and consequence. It loses confidence, most unnervingly, in the very words it is forced to go on speaking.

The experience is even more disorienting for being, day by day, upholstered with incidental pleasures and benefits. A great many of us in fact are living in the late 1970s more advantageously than we first expected to; direct injury and material dispossession are (within the class that writes and reads) less and less characteristic of individual life and fortune. Yet who now trusts this relative comfort or takes personal satisfaction in it? In a quite literal sense we find ourselves, as we look around, unable to define and pursue any private interest, or imagine taking part in any scheduled act or event, that cannot quickly enough be shown to have unbreakable connections with something elsewhere in the world that is intolerable to consciousness. We begin to see how everything that happens, everything it is now possible to satisfy personal curiosity about, can become an exclusionary advantage for some people and a cause of new misery for masses of others. And in the ever-widening gap between what incessantly presents itself to imaginative awareness and what in truth we are positioned and prepared to do in effective response, we risk paralysis even in reaching out no further than to those things we can directly touch and be touched by. It is as if human sensation itself had lost coherence, as if even this last fallback position in familiar experience had been overrun and annulled.

These framing circumstances of contemporary thought and work are outlined as efficiently as anywhere (within the limits of my own current reading) in an account by Fredric Jameson of the whole unprecedented modern situation.[19] Summarizing the writer's predicament under the cumulative pressure of modern life, Jameson formalizes a set of apprehensions which, though Marxist in a generalized sense, are not confined to a single ideological perspective. He speaks of an essential "fear and revulsion [the "fear and loathing" of current journalese] before the new and ever more systematized conditions of industrial society"; of "the atomization and disintegration of the older and more traditional collective groups and social modes"; of a profound and unnerving "split between public institutions and private experience"; and—psychologically, morally—of a "monadization and subjectification of individual existence," a "degradation" of personal life "to statistical anonymity, or to the status of mere case history." (Thus *privatization* and *depersonalization* go hand in glove.) The diagnosis will hardly be unfamiliar. Descriptions of the same prevailing conditions of life, more or less, have latterly become a kind of bookseller's commodity. I cite Jameson's because it is particularly compact yet offers something more than a mere recitation of symptoms, and because its further concern is with the consequences for the making of literature.*

The recognizable common truth in Jameson's account may considerably explain, in quite practical terms, our rising critical tolerance for the time-filling volubility that has returned to fashion. The reassurance of any sort of speaking voice, any unprogrammed personal utterance, becomes an end in itself, worth seeking out and giving one's ear to wherever found. Expectably, texts appealing to such tolerance are now commonplace. They accompany

*Not for the first time, speculative diagnosis has been richly anticipated in imaginative literature itself. Jameson's account, drawing in particular on Frankfurt School analysis, recapitulates Wordsworth's apprehension in the preface to the *Lyrical Ballads* of a "multitude of causes unknown to former times . . . now acting to blunt the discriminating powers of the mind and reduce it to a state of almost savage torpor." To Baudelaire, introducing the prose poems of *Le Spleen de Paris* a half-century later, the defining circumstance was the mind's defenselessness against the assault of modern city existence and its "crisscross of interconnections beyond number"; to Matthew Arnold it was simply "the strange disease of modern life." A hundred years forward, electronic metaphors have become dominant, as with the "roar of relays," the telephone dial's "ten million possibilities," the "twinned zeroes and ones" of a giant computer, in the last nightmare of the heroine of Pynchon's *The Crying of Lot 49*.

new publications on every level of assumed value as the very principle of their organization, or lack of it. Here, irresistible in its simplicity, is the introduction by the novelist Peter S. Beagle to a disposable work of subliterature published in 1975, pictures and letterpress, called *American Denim*: "I am for anything that says anything in a human voice," Beagle writes; "bumper stickers, decorated jeans, crazy T-shirts, even the strange small renaissance of tattooing. I am for talking, whatever form it takes. I am for voices."[20] At a higher intentional level the narrator of Joyce Carol Oates's *Expensive People* (1968) speaks to the same justifying principle as he launches upon his macabre deposition. Writing it out, he tells us, is not to be taken as an expression of artistic purposefulness on his part, nor a scheme for cash profit, nor even an act of confession seeking to establish credit of another sort. Rather it is life itself. "This story *is* my life"—a life he can't otherwise imagine himself continuing in. "It took me years to start writing this memoir, but now that I'm started, now that those ugly words are typed out, I could keep on typing forever."[21] (So he could—and so she does, Oates's detractors have been inclined to say as book after book has rolled out.) *Scribo ergo sum*.

Whatever the pathos and personal urgency of such motives, they appear to have, at least for authors, strict limits as a constitutive source. A literature that stakes everything on their potency is a literature likely to have lost confidence in any measure of effectiveness except personal relief, survivor's indemnification. Certainly it is one that has given up resisting, or even trying seriously to humanize, the long technological-institutional revolution of modern history; has given up attempting to legislate some antithetical collaborative order—the dream that for better or worse nourished the arts throughout the Romantic and modernist era.

Rather our literature presents itself as willing to accept a condition of imaginative servitude, willing even to embrace and help consolidate it if that is in fact how the historical wind blows. Perhaps the special respect accorded our newest Nobel laureate, Saul Bellow, whether or not each new novel satisfies expectation, derives from the rueful candor with which he acknowledges what is at stake, and what has already been given up, in the compromises writers are required to make in order to function at all. Bellow himself, as a novelist, has never pretended to stand clear of this servitude by playing spectacular formal and linguistic games with it or showily demonstrating that he knows all about it as a world-system. "To me," Bellow declared of his own *Herzog* (1964), and it is a comment belying his impatience elsewhere with the contemporary appetite for crisis language, "the significant theme is the imprisonment of the individual in a shameful and impotent privacy. He feels humiliated by it; he struggles comically with it; and he comes to realize at last that what he considered his intellectual's privilege has proved to be [only] another form of bondage."[22]

The double bind of this intuition—that the condition of being which stings you into counterstatement is the condition you must acquiesce in if you are to complete the work you have undertaken to do—provides the *déformation professionelle* which currently lies in wait for literary ambition in the old sense. And is commonly perceived as lying in wait. It is what denies to contemporary writing either the nourishment of great formal traditions (as these persist in the consciousness of actual audiences) or the hope of some liberating new covenant of legitimization. In times past the writer's license to participate in the "intellectual's privilege" has regularly been his mastery of a special repertory of qualities and resources by which the intractable chaos of experience might be subdued to the clarifications of significant form. But form, we now ask—the consummation of all incidental qualities—which is significant of exactly what, beyond its own self-seeking? And significant to whom, apart from an educated and bureaucratized elite holding on for dear life to illusions of cultural primacy and the satisfactions and prerogatives of commodity-market "excellence"? Bellow himself, in the text of *Herzog,* fixes on the collapse of these illusions when he identifies all certified poetic, philosophical, and religious thinking, the whole modern "dream of intellect," as no more than "a second realm of confusion"—and ends his novel, characteristically, in a gesture of relieved abnegation: "No messages [now] for anyone. Nothing. Not a single word."[23] Is it conceivable in the present age that the retreat from "qualities" and from the institutionalized complicity they involve us in can have, for literature itself, any different termination?

3

Bearing Witness, Negotiating Survival

The end of masterpieces . . . the beginning of testimony.
Robert Duncan, "Ideas of the Meaning of Form" (1961)

If we were concerned to characterize in a phrase the most accomplished American writing since the 1940s, we might call it a body of writing determined (in both senses: by choice and by compulsion) to *testify*, to bear direct witness to the personally apprehended life it rises from. This has meant first of all acknowledging the pain and degradation implicit in those shared conditions of life summarized in Fredric Jameson's account (discussed above, chapter two). Individual writers may or may not propose ideological explanations for what they are driven to say or for the cumulative judgments their work delivers. "Fear and loathing" can be disguised in various compensatory ways: not only in horror stories but in dreamlike visions of rescuing favored sectors of existence from the general ruin, or in fantasies of a power of resistance and escape within the grasp of certain exceptional groupings of persons. But whether or not the conveyed message is intentional and whether or not it is made fully explicit, we will find it stamped on the text. Has there been, for example, a more precise rendering of the circumstances Jameson evokes than, halfway through our period, John Updike's *Rabbit, Run* of 1960, in the account it too develops, but quite without sociological underscoring, of the "atomization and disintegration" of all the old supports to personal life: family, work, marriage, neighborhood and community, church and common faith? That is the burden, equally, of the novel's classically simple story and of nearly every one of those passages of miniscule description Updike falls back on in filling out its narrative space. (Small wonder that Mailer, though irritated by the literary-establishment flavor of *Rabbit, Run*'s prose, decided that among contemporaries it was Updike who appeared to have the surest instincts for finding the heartland of the novel proper.)[1]

The same basis for valuation seems to me to underlie the extraordinary critical welcome accorded, in 1974–1975, the oral autobiography of a black sharecropper, narrated under the protective pseudonym Nate Shaw, which came into existence as a book only through a series of fortunate accidents yet provides a solid measure of the achievement of more conventionally produced literature. Admiration for the narrative's sustained vividness of style and incident was touchingly reinforced by gratitude that a man had somehow survived through the whole modern era for whom family, neighborhood, work, church, marriage, and genuine personality did positively exist; a man who seemed to have undergone no such phenomenal split between public and private experience. Like a "black Homer" indeed, as reviewers spoke of him, Nate Shaw had been able to hold in mind the full story of his life, keeping track of the names, lineage, position, and character of more than four hundred other people, and tell that story out with a rare coherence when the time came, having against brutal odds remained free to store it in mind and tell and retell it throughout his days.[2]

It is true that he did so from inside a pastoral enclave where literacy and its equivocal interruptions were fragmentary at best, and world wars and ideological debates, and civil freedom, and justice, were for the most part unintelligible rumors. But the book's pastoralism is one that encompasses not only the peculiar restrictions of race but also—not a bit less than, say *Jennie Gerhardt* or *The Great Gatsby*— the special disturbances and liberations of the automobile age and the twentieth century's magnifying cycles of capitalist-imperialist disorder. (For Nate Shaw the First World War chiefly meant cotton at forty cents, not five, and hence a widening margin of security and incentive; and though illiterate he could, before the Depression canceled white forbearance, own and operate Herbert Hoover's two cars as well as a truck for heavier carrying.) In good times and bad the world of Nate Shaw—jailed in his midforties for joining a Communist-led union, and defended and, while in prison, pensioned by Stalinists of the International Labor Defense committee—was never exempt from the violences of modern political and economic dislocation.

These two first instances, *Rabbit, Run* and *All God's Dangers,* have more than a little in common in their imaginative formation. Updike himself has been something of an anachronism among younger writers after 1950 in having, like Nate Shaw, grown to adult consciousness in the same town and household where his grandparents lived and died, and with an apprehension of place and relationship nourished in the same unfractured temporal plenitude.[3] It is hard to think of a contemporary case quite like it (one not unreconstructibly provincial) even among southern and women writers. It seems against the grain of current probability, so disposed are we to think of displacement and alienation as preconditions of effective understanding. And perhaps the anachronism of it has turned out, for Updike, to be an imaginative limitation as well—though to my novel-reader's judgment the pace and detail in the best of his chronicles of how contemporary Pennsylvanians and New Englanders really act in each other's presence expose something self-enclosed and unseeing in the effort of nearly every other American novelist of major ambition over the past quarter century.

To propose this view of a Nate Shaw's or a John Updike's particular effectiveness is not to insist that good writing can come only from those whose sensibilities are rooted in an inherited, immediately experienced order of communal life and relationship. Neither is it to say that art necessarily turns false when it builds on ideological purposefulness and abstraction, although it has been our American-

antinomian inclination to think so. Most notable European fiction from *Rameau's Nephew* to *Doctor Zhivago*, and perhaps all great painting, would suggest otherwise. But when for the individual writer such purposefulness is in hostage to some severe original deprivation of relational experience—the order of experience, as Piaget tells us, that preeminently conditions our emergence as persons into the actual world—and when it expresses not only a will to exorcize this condition of deprivation but an unappeasable personal resentment at having been from so far back its unwitting victim, the writing that results may do no more than intensify the imaginative consequences, tightening their grip on writer and reader alike.

This particular nexus of private motive is what seems to me to unsettle at the core (more this than overproduction: a modernist fault, a Victorian virtue) Joyce Carol Oates's formidable attempt to grapple directly with the destructive atomization of contemporary life, and to give proper recognition to all the disregarded "other Americas" which are relentlessly victimized by it.[4] Putting fiction to such uses is an old and honorable undertaking for literary realists in general and for the modern religion of humanity most of them have thought to serve. But much more than with Dreiser early in the century, or even James T. Farrell around 1930, the murderous antagonisms Oates is determined to record seem in the end to overwhelm her imaginative judgment and her very considerable storytelling intelligence. The title of the novel with which she fully emerged from a characteristically intense schooling in the technic of modern fiction seems indicative. It is the novel she titled *them* (1969), and the lower-case printing is itself symptomatic of her shocked vision and of her will to shock others into sharing it. There is a sense in which all her characters, and her readers too, are "them" to her; are approached from that humiliated privacy Saul Bellow undertook to define in *Herzog*. The virtual anonymity of these fictive "them," their exclusion from established cultural privilege and recognition, oppresses Oates not least because she finds herself as impotent as anyone else to overcome it, even in her writing. One may speculate that she fears such disconnectedness in herself, despite her copiousness and proven readability. Typically, in any event, she makes a point of presenting the story told in *them* as one with special claims on her attention (and thus on ours); a story accidentally delivered to her when for once the barrier dividing her life from the lives of the students she was teaching was broken through and conditions of contemporary existence normally unreported and inaccessible to report came to light. So in her own mind her first obligation as novelist was to take what she had discovered and force it past the incomprehension of that ordinary book-buying readership which appreciatively patronizes "good" writing and takes easy credit for its liberal cultivation in doing so.

There is, as one considers the case, an interesting convergence between Oates's calculatedly aggressive fiction and the equally purposeful and prolific writing of the social psychologist Robert Coles, whose work I would take as representative of a whole paraliterary class of messages to the age.* He too is honorably determined to bear witness to any number of disregarded "other Americas," and also to challenge very directly our liberal book reader's indifference to the shrinkages of life and hope each such undersociety is condemned to. There is a convergence also with the mid-career self-transformations of several gifted school poets—Adrienne Rich is a notable example—who have driven themselves into this same posture of accusatory public testimony. With Oates and Rich all the resources of a studious apprenticeship to modern literature, with Coles the corresponding authority of modern psychoanalytic and socioanthropological understanding, are marshaled (or else conspicuously rejected) for a purgative assault on their audience's complacency. In Coles's more recent writings in particular, as in Rich's latest poetry, this assault has frequently moved toward outright denunciation: of citizen-readers who hide out behind self-serving platitudes at a safe distance from the flashpoints of contemporary injustice, or else—in several homiletic studies Coles has devoted to morally favored authors

---

*A number of books in this general class have been separately categorized as "non-fiction novels," a genre of factual narration supposedly invented during the 1960s. The kind of book in question, however—such as Truman Capote's *In Cold Blood* (1964), Oscar Lewis's *La Vida* (1966), Mailer's *The Armies of the Night*, and Tom Wolfe's *The Electric Kool-Aid Acid Test* (both 1968)—does not seem to me either original with our era or formally in need of some specially designed mode of assessment. In any case this subgenre will not be separately discussed here.

like William Carlos Williams, James Agee, Georges Bernanos—of those more famous modernists, such as Joyce, who in their service to the idol art are alleged to have put aside their testamentary obligation to the disfranchised "them" of modern life.

As to the importance of the testimony thus flung at us, judgments may sharply divide. It is possible to be stirred by the basic complaint, and of course by the material evidence which earns it a hearing, and yet find ourselves in each instance raising the primitive and unavoidably ad hominem question of authenticity. For we may eventually feel that what each of these writers has to say is not anchored in an endorsing fullness of absorbed private experience but represents instead a kind of public and period ventriloquism, a straining to speak from elsewhere than that baffling inexperience and separateness whose persistence in the writer's own consciousness is a continuing source of chagrin and anger. Resenting a deprivation of sensibility in themselves—and how can they not, as responsible spirits?—they mean to forestall it or else punish it in others. But whatever the virtue of this intention, it forces the question (hardly for the first time in the history of literature): can you make imaginative truth out of the exposure and implicit denunciation of the intolerable inadvertence you assume in all your readers? At first, recognizing it as having been your own inadvertence as well, you may bring to it the saving authority of self-implication. You yourself are seen to have been shocked as a writer into a certain bald reactive truthfulness. After that, unfortunately, the technique can become as artificial as any other, and simply one more saleable literary commodity.

Yet in the rush of performance such writing can have the force it seeks. The effects gained are not illegitimate. Of Oates's narratives in particular, with their old-fashioned naturalistic underlining, is this true. Whether she writes to compensate for all the grotesque violations of hope and need that surround her and surround us all, or to justify the comparable violence of an unappeasable *ressentiment*—whether, that is, she writes as witness or as victim—hardly matters if we take her at her own pace and imaginative measure. If the Detroit, Houston, Buffalo of the 1950s, 1960s, and 1970s were to dream collectively, they would dream, I think, something very close to a Joyce Carol Oates novel.

With regard to the determining focus of our concern with literature that I argued for (all too briefly) in the first chapter—the question of how human beings, in their separate capacities, actively coexist in the world—two basic kinds of testimony may be said to dominate American writing since the 1940s. The literary modes they result in are, at a glance, different in the extreme. On one side we find long, minutely circumstantial prose fictions tending to be fantastic in outlook and specification, yet naturalistic in their cumulative progressions, their formalized interpretation of motive and consequence. On the other side, what typically materializes is a poetry of lyric self-absorption and self-projection, a poetry shaped in expression to essentially anecdotal repetitions of private impulse and feeling; most frequently, it may seem, of private frustration. But in the kinds of statement each mode is capable of, they seem essentially complementary. They are the two sides of one traumatic coinage; and what they advertise is a practice of literature that cannot find voice or even define an effective ambition without more or less abjectly surrendering itself to the collective nightmares that have shocked it into being.

2

> Paranoia strikes deep....
> The Buffalo Springfield (1966)

Fiction first. When the second-generation Paris expatriates described by Mordecai Richler began in the 1950s to make capital of their after-hours diversions, they borrowed or parodied various subliterary modes of their American adolescence: movie and radio scripts, comic books of the Captain Marvel era, detective and spy stories, horror fantasies—how many were H. P. Lovecraft addicts?—science fiction, and the like. These popular modes all have one formal element in common (one they share with the complex of attitudes we associate with American populism). It is simply that nothing ever happens in them which is not understood to be part of some governing scheme or counterscheme of manipulation and control. No signal, no observed occurrence, lacks its purposeful agent or hidden source; consequently, no action takes place without a fully programmed motive and without incurring an equal and opposite narrative reaction, until the final hair-breadth triumph or escape of the program-obedient yet miraculously changeless hero.

Nothing, in short, is contingent or accidental. A kind of double-entry, zero-sum narrative economics prevails, and anyone squandering energy on merely personal impulse and feeling is invariably made a fool of or a fall guy, someone to be sacrificed to the system as a whole—precisely as, in the totalizing vision of superpower politics, mavericks and misfits are always to be sacrificed to the central struggle for domination and control. This has been, indeed, the persistent narrative logic of trade books openly exploiting the apocalypse-prone fears and wishes of mass consciousness, from populist political romances like Ignatius Donnelly's *Caesar's Column* (1891) and Jack London's *The Iron Heel* (1907) to Cold War entertainments in the fashion, cartoon-satire crossbred with science fiction, of Kurt Vonnegut's *Player Piano* (1952) and *The Sirens of Titan* (1959).* It is also the fundamental narrative logic of an extended series of novels which have been the prizewinners and cult successes of the last two decades of American writing; novels asserting the existence (or their characters' paralyzing belief in the existence) of some immense, bureaucratized, conspiratorial *system* to which men and women are essentially enslaved, whether they know it or not, and from which no escape is possible except by a withdrawal of selfhood so absolute that its natural fulfillment is suicide.

This is the familiar category of the conspiracy

*The same logic stands at the mythopoeic core of Henry James's quasi-political novel, *The Princess Casamassima* (1886).

novel—or, reversing the spyglass, the novel of paranoia—which, in surveying American fiction of the 1950s and 1960s, Tony Tanner and others have rightly picked out for special emphasis.[5] It will be worth reviewing the titles and main situations of some of the most expert within this category; for if we have to do here with a single imaginative fixation, it is one that has found expression in an ingenious variety of forms:

—in Joseph Heller's *Catch-22* (1961) the conspiratorial system is the whole perfect and unassailable enterprise of modern war, and it is defined, typically, in terms of madness; you can't break out of it unless you are certified as crazy, but you can't get certified as crazy if you value life enough to try seriously to break out;*

—in Ken Kesey's *One Flew over the Cuckoo's Nest* (1961) it is the asylum dictatorship of the terrifying Big Nurse; here again the system of subjugation becomes, in operation, self-perpetuating;[6]

—in John Barth's *Giles Goat-Boy* (1966) it is the tediously elaborated West Campus system, mirroring the totalitarian organization of contemporary life, its universities included, for service in a permanent Cold War;

—in a parallel example from theater, Edward Albee's *The American Dream* (1960), it is simply the

*It is a system oddly replicated in the way language itself is made to operate in *Catch-22*, especially in conversations between its type-frozen characters. As in the formalized stychomythia of burlesque-show dialogue, anything that the linguistic patterns regularly in use in the book allow one to say *will* get said in due course, whether or not it makes sense.

mutilating tyranny of the ordinary American family, Mummy and Daddy at the controls; a subsociety Thornton Wilder had warmly idealized a generation earlier, but one whose essential rites, we now learn, are infanticide and premature euthanasia;

—in Vonnegut's *Cat's Cradle* (1963) it is symbolized by the ultimate comic-book weapon, Ice-Nine, and also by the doubly comforting theology of Bokononism: "We Bokononists believe that humanity is organized into teams, teams that do God's will without ever discovering what they are doing";[7]

—in Robert Stone's workmanlike novels, *A Hall of Mirrors* (1967) and *Dog Soldiers* (1975), it is the symbiotic drug-traffic, crime-syndicate, police-squad system which in the era of the Vietnam War is seen expanding into the highest reaches of national policy;

—in Mailer's *An American Dream* (1965) the idea of institutionalized conspiracy provides the smokescreen, again at the level of national policy, by means of which the congressman-protagonist effectively keeps the police from investigating the power-trip murder he commits early in the novel;

—in Vladimir Nabokov's *Pale Fire* (1962) it is fundamental, as a prepared narrative *topos*, to the book's unresolvable ambiguities of specification (*did* a poet named John Shade really exist? *is* there a distant northern land called Zembla where murderous plotting and counterplotting are the chief business of state?); fundamental also to our enjoyment of the compositional sleight-of-hand Nabokov is intent on performing;

—in John A. Williams's *The Man Who Cried I Am* (1967) the same fixation emerges, not less ambiguously, in allegations of a vast conspiracy against the black population of the entire world;[8]

—and in what may be the purest and, among writers, most influential case of all, it creates the boundaryless network of control comprising the drug addict's vision of William Burroughs's *Naked Lunch* (1959).

Interestingly, Burroughs's repellent novel, first in this series to reach print, is the one that spells out most plainly the laws of existence that all of them assume. In *Naked Lunch* total design and total chaos become twin objectifications of the same fantastic fear. Modern bureaucracy is its familiar institutionalized form, the "complete cellular representation" that is our society's distinctive "cancer"; and there is a frequently remarked irony in Burroughs's being himself the black-sheep heir to a business-machine fortune. But the self-perpetuating, worldwide drug traffic is the system's real *raison d'être* as well as its root metaphor. "There are no accidents in the junk world," Burroughs writes. Certainly it is not accidental that "the Man is never on time," abject physical anguish being essential to the totally coercive agency of deprivation. Correspondingly, individual feelings and actions, and human speech itself, lose all meaning or consequence: "The same things said a million times and more, and there is no point in saying anything because NOTHING *Ever Happens* in the junk world." (The same sterility is expressed in Burroughs's complementary addiction to homosexual overspill and the violent exclusion of women.) And there is this one further rule, as degrading as the worst captive-mind nightmare of the Hitler-Stalin era, that under addiction's terrible "algebra of need" the final truth about every natural human relationship will be the truth of personal betrayal, or of a dehumanizing readiness to betray: "You would lie, cheat, inform on your friends, steal, *do anything* to satisfy total need."[9] The more horrific details of "biocontrol" imagined in the later volumes of the *Naked Lunch* tetralogy add nothing to the absoluteness of this projected surrender of full intersubjective selfhood.

No doubt we are more inclined now than when these books began to appear to grant them a degree of realism, perhaps even a broad figural truth. It has become a sociologist's truism to point out how naturally the themes of conspiracy and paranoia rise from the experience of certain classes within the organizational network of modern life, where institutional programming and personal meaninglessness are more and more apprehended as the universal rule.[10] The same themes issue for self-evident reasons from the entire historical experience of black Americans under the mystifying coercions of racism, which teach that there is no human relationship whatsoever that cannot be assimilated into the system of domination and personal betrayal. Thus these themes enter quite naturally the fiction of Richard Wright and Ralph Ellison, among others, in the 1940s and 1950s—though it needs also to be said that the core strength of the stories told in *Native Son*

(1940) and *Black Boy* (1945) and in *Invisible Man* (1952) has to do not only with their testamentary truthfulness but with both authors' perception that at some deep level, along those "lower frequencies" Ellison's hero claims access to, they are giving voice to an experience of life which potentially threatens all their readers.

For the same themes, the same consciousness of the rules of existence, rise equally naturally from the experience of any set of people who see that they are not to be allowed to act freely and consequentially in the world, according to promise and shared birthright. So this consciousness plays its decisive part, along with foredoomed fantasies of release and escape, in the closed imaginative world of women writers like Carson McCullers and Flannery O'Connor (much as it had with Edith Wharton, Willa Cather, Ellen Glasgow, earlier in the century).[11] It is correspondingly central to the child's or adolescent's vision that directs J. D. Salinger's storytelling, most memorably in *The Catcher in the Rye* (1951); as indeed it is to the novels and stories of that whole gallery of city-bred, second and third-generation Jewish writers from Nathanael West on, inheritors of a multiple cultural (and linguistic) dispossession, who have accounted for so large a share of our liveliest parable-testaments over the past forty-odd years.

Thus in each of Saul Bellow's first two novels the conspiracy and paranoia theme is knowingly exploited, the more effectively for having a natural place within a basically realistic field of action. At the end of *The Victim* (1948) the invincibly naive hero has one last question for his unrepentant tormentor: "Wait a minute," he calls out, "what's your idea of who runs things?" There the conflict and its ironies are essentially private—except of course as it involves the world disease of anti-Semitism. But in *Dangling Man* (1944), four years before the corresponding reversal which ends Orwell's *1984*, Bellow nailed down the narrative increment distinguishing these contemporary conspiracy tales from their mechanistic forerunners; and that is the interiorization of the whole system of control in a clinching act of personal consent, of voluntary self-betrayal. The ordeal of Bellow's Kafkan hero, waiting for the Army's summons, ends in a very ecstacy of submission:

I am no longer to be held accountable for myself [B. writes in his journal]; I am grateful for that. I am in other hands, relieved of self-determination, freedom canceled.
Hurray for regular hours!
And for the supervision of the spirit!
Long live regimentation!

—a coda reduced, two wars later, to even greater succinctness by Mailer's disk-jockey narrator in *Why Are We in Vietnam?* (1967): "Vietnam! Hot damn!"[12]

But the largest class of all to be caught up in these numbing apprehensions is simply the whole literature-producing, fiction-consuming middle and literate class in modern society. No specifically Marxist standpoint is required to see that, in longer perspective, the mass of our recent fiction only adds a further, relatively undifferentiated chapter to the familiar chronicle of middle-class disaffection and alienation—alienation from that very organization of life, with its material rewards and social privilege, which this class's historical triumph brought into being. Money itself, the simplifying currency (literally) of bourgeois social exchange, is after all the ultimate conspiratorial force, the invisible hand reaching into every life relationship. The venture-capital American faith in a new birth of freedom and new order of the ages intensifies and concentrates these ironies of alienation when they occur. The brighter and more nearly universal the original hope, the more enormous the trauma of disillusion, and the conviction of some huge betrayal. If there has been, in Richard Hofstadter's formula, a "paranoid style in American politics" and a chronic persuasion that treasonous conspiracies are the ground and purpose of every objectionable policy or circumstance, it is not surprising to find the same paranoia encapsulated in popular fiction.

Yet I think a review of recent and current fiction carried out at the end of the 1950s would have established a rather different basic emphasis. It would surely have turned up the same repeated insistence on the experience of dispossession and alienation— for which it could also have adduced a distinguished literary ancestry; one not limited, of course, to American titles. But would the collective testimony assembled have been quite so monotone and bleakly despairing? With books like *Invisible Man* and *The Catcher in the Rye,* Eudora Welty's *The Golden Apples* (1949), Wright Morris's *Love Among the Cannibals*

(1957), Barth's *The End of the Road* (1958) or even Kerouac's *On the Road* (1957), or with Bellow's *Seize the Day* (1956) and certainly with *Henderson the Rain King* at the decade's end, just as with "Bartleby the Scrivener" or *Huckleberry Finn*, *Gatsby* or *The Wild Palms* in earlier periods, a measurably different impression materializes. There is, first, the writer's own infectious "courage of treatment" (Emerson's phrase, again, for *Leaves of Grass*); his determination not to slide off into cartoon-strip fantastication but to project and substantiate a world of experience that corresponds in minute particulars to the one we all inwardly know or might know. And there is also, on the writer's part, a basic generosity toward his leading characters; an admiration for some off-center vitality and integrity of being that brings them alive to him in the first place (embodying the energy of invention he feels in himself); a receptive patience and attentiveness in allowing them to maneuver on their own terms even when, as commonly happens, they crash on down to defeat.

The narrative result of these working attitudes is not the cool, distanced tabulation of outrage upon outrage that characterizes the bulk of sixties fiction, but a tangible endorsement of the wanderings and evasions of living personality.*[13] By this means,

*In archetypal terms the chief instrument for expressing this confidence in active personality remains, interestingly, the trickster tale; a staple, as one might guess, of black fiction in particular, from Langston Hughes's good-tempered "Simple" stories to the pugnacities of Amiri Baraka's "black arts" movement. The bad karma of the world of power and control is offset, one way or another, by the protagonist's repertory of counterdevices. In

movement and change come into the written narrative sequence, in contrast to the rule of irreversible predetermination in novels where the control system itself is the real protagonist, the preemptive agent of all that takes place. And nothing, I would argue, is more important to our willingness to believe, or to suspend disbelief, in the story we are being asked to re-create in imagination; for is not some corresponding perception of movement and change, of *actantial* succession and difference, basic to our apprehension as persons of the continuum of actual life?* Basic, that is, to our way of knowing anything in the world. So it is in general—as Sartre argued in *What Is Literature?*—that fiction works to recover the

---

Jack Kerouac's definition of the hipster the same folk-archetype is re-created, but with a notable difference from Burroughs's monochrome version (whether or not it is a difference that convinces). To Kerouac—in John Tytell's summary—the hipster is the man who can always get drugs, and who moreover can get them on his own terms. He is the "marginal man" who nevertheless understands "how to penetrate the cosmopolitan center, with a ken for its rules and an instinct for self-preservation" (John Tytell, *Naked Angels: The Lives and Literature of the Beat Generation* [New York: McGraw-Hill, 1976], pp. 22–23). The confrontation in Kerouac's fictional vision of open road and corrupting cosmopolitan center may remind us that we are also dealing here with archetypes of American pastoralism.

*Actantial translates A. J. Greimas's Kenneth-Burkean (and Aristotelian) word *actant* for the fundamental element of *doing* and *making happen* in narrative construction. It strikes me as one of the relatively few coinages of recent French theorizing which fills a gap in our own critical terminology—as opposed, for instance, to *différence*, which merely scholasticizes the self-evident fact that phenomena catch our attention only as they deviate from the attentive fix they intrude upon.

phenomenal world, "by giving it to be seen as it is, but as if it had its source in human freedom."[14]

One narrative paradigm common to these novels of the late 1940s and the 1950s deserves fuller comment, because it embraces the crucial *topos* of betrayal. In nearly every one of the novels just cited a relationship between important characters is proposed that is held to be exempt from the mechanisms of servitude and domination controlling life as a whole; that taps instead some free, animating reserve of natural feeling. These exempted relationships are likely to be random and unstable at best. Essentially accidental, they have no enduring power to transcend, let alone overcome, the general regimen. In a pattern Leslie Fiedler was the first to trace systematically through our grandest fiction, they regularly encroach on central taboos of incest, homosexuality, parricide, and race[15]—and like the friendship in *On the Road* between Sal Paradise and Dean Moriarity, these relationships invariably end or threaten to end in just those acts of personal betrayal they are most anxiously in flight from. Yet the characters in question are not finally broken in will or hope. They remain, in ways Eudora Welty attributes to the general class of "wanderers" in *The Golden Apples*, men and women who—even when life does at last yield moments of sweetness and fulfillment—are not quite satisfied; who "always [wish] for a little more of what had just been"; yet for whom life's returning "attrition," though not to be escaped, may finally distill its portion of "wisdom."[16]

Which is to say that in these novels and stories of twenty and thirty years ago the traps with which modern history negates its illusory promise of private freedom are all baited and ready to spring. Contemporary society's machines for disseverance and degradation remain aggressively at work. But for a time at least, certain characters are seen as acting more or less resourcefully against them—and the writer's own surprising resourcefulness in furnishing a corroborative syntax of gesture and speech makes these countermovements fictionally persuasive.

It is interesting to discover Saul Bellow, in 1952, praising *Invisible Man* in just such terms. Bellow's review, written for *Commentary,* began by assuming as a matter of course the immense plausibility of the whole conspiratorial vision—the subjection of human life to some programmed system of domination, and coincidentally, for the arts, a necessary end to individual efficacy and freedom in the traditional sense:

> It is commonly felt that there is no strength to match the strength of those powers which attack and cripple modern mankind. And this feeling is, for the reader of modern fiction, all too often confirmed when he approaches a new book. He is prepared, skeptically, to find what he has found before, that family and class, university, fashion, the giants of publicity and manufacture, have had a larger share in the creation of someone called a writer than truth or imagination—that Bendix and Studebaker and the nylon division of DuPont, and the University of Chicago, or Columbia or Harvard or Kenyon College, have once more proved mightier than the single soul of an individ-

ual.... But what a great thing it is when a brilliant individual victory occurs, like Mr. Ellison's, proving that a truly heroic quality can exist among our contemporaries. People too thoroughly determined—and our institutions by their size and force too thoroughly determine—can't approach this quality.

And Bellow went on, unerringly, to offer as proof of "the very strongest sort of creative intelligence" the episode in which the incestuous black sharecropper, Trueblood, mesmerizes a credulous white philanthropist with a circumstantial re-creation of his tabooed crime of crimes.[17] That the example chosen is not in fact a stroke of pure invention on Ellison's part only confirms Bellow's larger argument. Like more than one of *Invisible Man*'s vivid pageant of scenes, Trueblood's long recital derives from well-established oral tradition. It has as many tellings behind it, and as much anonymous amplification and refinement, as the Dauphin's camp-meeting jape in *Huckleberry Finn* or as the poet Etheridge Knight's ebullient re-creation of the famous "Titanic" toast. Ellison's "brilliant individual victory" in *Invisible Man*—a novel whose resourcefulness of voice overrides its kaleidoscopic organization—largely results from opening his narrative to materials and speech patterns which, when he wrote, lay mostly outside regular literary use, yet had been cut and polished by generations of unmonitored speech-exchange.

It is just such naturalness in the preparation— Emerson's "long foreground"—that seems missing in the newer 1960s mode of overdetermined conspiracy-and-paranoia fiction. This mode may in any case have reached a self-devouring climax in Pynchon's prize-winning *Gravity's Rainbow* (1973), a novel which, whether or not it initially balked consecutive reading in the degree reported even by admiring reviewers, appears now to have settled into place as, among contemporary superfictions, one of the least re-readable.[18] It is, beyond question, an extraordinary construct, a *tour de force* of textual assemblage. The contemporary information-retrieval novel has, to date, no more imposing monument. Certainly with its multiple layerings of lecture-course and newspaper-file facticity it is a weightier achievement than such other recent exercises in historiographic re-creation as E. L. Doctorow's *Ragtime* and Gore Vidal's *Burr* and *1876,* or than Pynchon's own scenario-novel *V.* (1963); books which, though well deserving their season of popularity, slide elegantly but frictionlessly in and out of mind.

Yet the prose text of *Gravity's Rainbow* seems to me—to put the case against it all too bluntly—one which lacks a serious fiction's essential fidelity to a reciprocated human norm. The oddness of the book's angle of vision is not at issue. The surreal in literature can render its meanings as seriously as any other mode. It is rather the basic manner of the rendering, page by page, that frustrates acceptance. As a narrative fiction *Gravity's Rainbow* seems less written than programmed. Its constituent events and persons (and their personalized delusions) cast no affective shadow of their own; they exist only to serve the preconceived mechanism of the whole. Beyond their first specification they are allowed no interior power to modify or reorder the book's field of imaginative action, which remains fixed throughout, immured against second thoughts—though it is powerful enough as first conceived, with its projection of a mysterious Central European "Zone" where a new, transmogrified order of historical existence gradually reveals its features. Within this unconditioned field of action individual characters are only so many interchangeable ciphers. They are shuffled into place and assigned their comic-strip names only for what can be done *to* them, for the humiliations which are to be inflicted *on* them.

And all occurs within a systematization of existence that the writer has not so much proposed for exploration as submitted his inventiveness to at every turn. So, too, the metaphor of gravity itself, including the rocket dream of breaking free of it, can only be submitted to in the design of the whole. No dynamic of relation is allowed into the book which operates apart from that unitary rule of falling bodies.* Even more completely than the world of

---

*The duplication in *Gravity's Rainbow* of Henry Adams's experiments in applying the conceptions of physics to modern history has been widely noted. For Adams, however, scientific laws were ultimately symbols of a kind of knowledge regrettably unavailable to chroniclers of human actions. To suppose otherwise was an act of credulousness not different in kind from any magical shortcut.

For this whole class of fictions positing behavioral control systems, a nearer correspondence is with the popular ethological literature of the 1960s and 1970s, books categorizing human behavior in terms of one or another evolutionary instinct as unvarying as gravity and as irreversible as physical entropy: ag-

experience projected in *V.* (about which Tony Tanner has remarked that authentic inter-subjectivity has all but vanished),[19] the putative human world in *Gravity's Rainbow* has been replaced by descriptive hypotheses about such a world. Since such description is logically endless, the detail of it may be endlessly improvised and multiplied, yet never move across into any sphere of verification answering to the cognitive or affective circumstance of our own relation-multiplying lives.[20]

What this results in can be described—not, I think, unfairly or necessarily without due admiration—as cosmology rather than answerable narrative. *Gravity's Rainbow* stands as the latest paragnostic attempt to give an independent material and formal basis to imaginative states that in truth (and also, as I uncertainly understand the matter, in logic) cannot be separated from the progressions of spirit and will they rise from in ordinary life. As a printed text the book can feel, if you give your mind to it, quite powerful as an expression of recognizable contemporary obsessions, and as an immense ritual charm against them. Yet I doubt very much whether

---

gression (Lorenz), territoriality (Ardrey), species bonding (Tiger and Fox), appetite reinforcement (Skinner), erotic repression and the death drive (Norman O. Brown), and the like. In both forms it seems more than just possible that the concealed message is a radical diminution, if not suspension, of political will. On actual civil issues like black equality, Mr. Robert Ardrey remains, quite admirably, a principled 1930s liberal. But since the 1930s the older liberalism has been hard put to maintain its necessary quantum of confidence, and has taken to the manufacturing of hyperbolic excuses as a way of covering its huge disappointment.

it will prove to have any continuing importance in literary history—and there seems to me some point in trying to understand why this is predictably the case.

I would take it as basic to all we willingly keep track of as literature (distinguishing it from scripture or scientific treatise), all we read for other than utilitarian or pharmacological reasons, that the world of human and historical experience, as in feeling and through language we commonly know it, is *not* identical with the physical energy system of material creation; a system which, even as it inheres in our own physical being, we cannot *know* but only *know about*, in progressively less remote and absurd analytical simulations. Neither are the sequences of what has moral weight and force for us, the sequences of everything we are not free in human nature to remain uncaring about, comparable to the chemical structure of carbon rings—to cite a representative analogy in *Gravity's Rainbow*. They are not in fact ring-like at all: that is, unvaryingly concentric, symmetrical, repetitive and self-enclosed. But Pynchon's text does not, as I make it out, admit any other presentational perspective, either in its own descriptive voice or in satirizing and parodying the delusions of its cipher-characters. I hope the burden of these reservations will not be misunderstood. By every incidental test the intelligence at work in *Gravity's Rainbow* is exceptionally vigorous and intense. But it has all the qualities of an intelligence stuck fast—"brilliantly" stuck, to be sure—at the threshold of those obsessive, distinction-effacing perceptions of universal analogy which increasingly in the cruel expansions of modern knowledge have been pressed into service to cover the sense of an immense weakening of intellectual control, of moral and practical imagination; a weakening of which, given its origins in the whole merciless economy of modern life, a first consequence must be that no one in particular is at fault or to blame.*

(But one further critical point needs to be made, which is that the problem *Gravity's Rainbow* presents to judgment is also, and perhaps centrally, a problem of style. Deliberately or not, Pynchon's narrative style in this book seems all too perfectly in keeping with the reductions and exclusions of its brutalizing historical vision.[21] The novel's incremental freightage of reference and allusion is indeed encyclopedic in scope, but it is also encyclopedically monotonous and static. Its constituent sentences seem to me as inert, as they fall out on the page, as its gallery of characterizations, and have the same assembly-line flatness and tonelessness. Starting with that celebrated overture—"A screaming comes across the sky": a sentence lending itself all too easily

---

*A second consequence, within the field of Pynchon's novel, is that everyone must suffer the same uniformly degrading personal fate, the same total loss of self-determination. *Gravity's Rainbow* may indeed be the novel that "qualitatively subsumes everything that has happened since its putative action of 1944–45," as Lawrence C. Wolfley has recently asserted ("Repression's Rainbow: The Presence of Norman O. Brown in Pynchon's Big Novel," *PMLA*, October 1977, p. 888n). But such claims leave untouched the crucial objection that the book's own system of narrative registration cannot itself be seen as anything but self-feeding and self-repetitive.

to the uses of jacket copy—they are interposed like advertising-agency sentences between the reader and the imaginable content of the situations and events they detail. The least intelligible comments on *Gravity's Rainbow* in the springtime euphoria of its first reception were those celebrating its beauty and humor of style and making talismanic comparisons to the narrative prose of Melville and Faulkner.)

In placing Pynchon's book in the full context of contemporary American fiction, Roger Sale has proposed the category of the "American imperial novel," our fiction's counterpart to the total-control, data-process thinking that took charge of American foreign policy in the early 1960s. As it happens, the actual taste in fiction of the new-model American president who came to power in 1961 is said to have run to a simpler, more stereotyped kind of novelistic war gaming, specifically the James Bond fantasies of Ian Fleming. Is it altogether absurd to suggest that reading *Gravity's Rainbow* as a vast amalgam of these two closed operational systems—a James Bond adventure redesigned for total victory (over villains, heroes, and innocent bystanders alike) by an unusually persistent and model-obsessed tactical planning team—is not to miss the core of meaning the book builds out from? For the text is one that from the title forward imaginatively endorses the removal of historical actions from any commonly accessible realm of judgment and responsibility. It does this as thoroughly as it reduces private conduct to a mechanical programming, and reflective intelligence to a stenciling of predetermined response patterns.

These are reductions, to be sure, which modern political experience has made nightmarishly plausible. They are the uncontrollable specters of our era's most general fear. But I would contend that a narrative text which is conceived, even in legitimate comic insolence, as a printout simulation of some such unitary field-structure of history and nature combined can have no durable hold on our natural interest in human and historical existence, in either its largest or its smallest configurations; no more than an epileptic seizure, though remarkable to observe and furnishing information perhaps not otherwise to be obtained, can take hold as a first measure of functioning human consciousness.

Such a text becomes at best one of those essentially self-nullifying productions of contemporary writing Roland Barthes has described in *Le Plaisir du texte,* productions which can be everything to consciousness but fertilizing. These are texts, Barthes writes, that "exhaust their necessity as soon as they have been seen, since to see them is immediately to understand to what destructive purpose they are exhibited: they no longer contain any *contemplative* or *delectative* duration" (my emphasis). Essentially sterile in operation, voyeurist and self-obstructed, their governing vision is one that "can only repeat itself—without ever introducing anything."[22]

In contrast, the American fiction written since the 1940s that best continues to hold interest and give reflective pleasure commonly follows a more conventional discipline of workmanship. The best of it will be found, I think, in a series of books which are on a noticeably more modest scale but in which we sense that the writer's own most intimate apprehension of life stands directly behind everything presented.* Imaginative compression and a severe narrative economy are a first sign of this saving discipline. None of them is a Great American Novel (though nearly all are by writers who at some point during these years did try their hand, less successfully, at a big book aiming at some more panoramic revelation or truth). Their overform is rather that of the *novella,* which traditionally, in E. K. Bennett's classic formula, lends itself to the intensive elaboration of some one particular "situation, conflict, event, or aspect of personality."[23] Pynchon himself, it should be said, has written one of the most original and stylish in this series. *The Crying of Lot 49* is that one of his three books, to date, in which conception and execution seem thoroughly in balance and the improvised detail keeps deftly to the measure of what imagina-

---

*The series I have in mind runs from McCullers's "The Ballad of the Sad Café" (1944; 1951), Salinger's *The Catcher in the Rye* (1951), O'Connor's *Wise Blood* (1952), William Styron's *The Long March* (1952), Wright Morris's *The Deep Sleep* (1953), James Baldwin's *Go Tell It On the Mountain* (1953), Bellow's *Seize the Day* (1956), Bernard Malamud's *The Assistant* (1957), Nabokov's *Pnin* (1957) and also, perhaps, *Bend Sinister* (1947), to William H. Gass's "The Pedersen Kid" (1961), Walker Percy's *The Moviegoer* (1961), John A. Williams's *Sissie* (1963), Updike's *The Centaur* (1963), Pynchon's *The Crying of Lot 49* (1966), Mailer's *Why Are We in Vietnam?* (1967), Welty's *The Optimist's Daughter* (1972). I don't mean this list to be canonical. Additions are welcome, and I grant whatever further authority goes with the greater mass and scale of novels like *Invisible Man, Lolita,* or *Henderson the Rain King*—but I am confident about the particular judgments of compositional effectiveness it derives from.

tion has grasped at first hand. Paranoia and universal conspiracy remain his organizing themes, but their fictive development serves a plausible sequence of action—the step-by-step progress of his ingratiatingly average heroine, Oedipa Maas (nervy, likable, generous-spirited), into the gimcrack labyrinth of contemporary middle-class hallucination.

3

> A thousand people in the street,
> Singin' songs and carryin' signs. . . .
> The Buffalo Springfield (1966)

For poets the measure of direct personal consciousness is harder to evade, harder also to transpose into some more general truthfulness of statement. Since the early 1950s a certain imperialization of purpose and design has run its course in American poetry, too, as if seeking, in a dangerous time, the same compensatory increase of power that our control-system novelists have grasped for. What it has given us, particularly over the past decade, is a series of outsized, loosely assembled, quasi-universal books laying out the poet's personal apprehensions within some large interpretive synthesis, or else proceeding on the assumption that a legitimizing synthesis is bound to materialize sooner or later. What you have to do as poet is keep working along and leave the text open to whatever expressive notions and linkages happen to show up in your elected field of argument, in the order in which they come.

These book-length poems are not exclusively the work of disciples of Pound and Charles Olson. But the *Cantos* have been, for most, the major justifying model, with their inordinate dream of securing for everything one might admire in recorded human life, and wish to be associated with, the fixedness equally of carved stone and of metamorphic recurrence; and *The Maximus Poems* (1953–1968), renewing in contemporary terms the familiar American *pietas* of locality and private occupation, stand directly behind projects like Robert Kelly's *The Common Shore* (1969) and Edward Dorn's *Gunslinger* (1968–1972), to mention only the most handsomely produced. Yet Lowell's *History* in its first unsorted form had much the same structural logic, or lack of it—as for that matter did Williams's overprepared bid for mastery in *Paterson* (1946–1958): beautifully worked fragments within an unrealized epic scheme. Correspondingly, nothing generated inside the work itself explains why Robert Penn Warren's *Or Else* (1974) is presented as "a single long poem"; whereas George Keithley's *The Donner Party* (1972) and James Merrill's "The Book of Ephraim" (1976) do clearly project a continuous narrative sequence, and Donald Finkel's *Adequate Earth* (1972), rather artificially offering its "messages, readings, observations" within a framework of Antarctic exploration, at least recognizes the advantages of simulating one. But in A. R. Ammons's *Tape for the Turn of the Year* (1965) and *Sphere* (1973), inconsequence and shapelessness seem to have become regulating principles. Length and bulk (as David Bromwich has noted, reviewing Ammons) now appear to justify whatever is introduced to achieve them.[24]

The relative failure of most of these projects to convince even a favorably disposed reader that they are more than assemblages of fragments derives less, I suspect, from failures of expressive stamina than from the intransigent demands of poetry itself; more exactly, from the demands we continue to bring to the mode of poetic statement, despite much ingenious countertheorizing. We still count on poetry, however unconventional or perhaps "decreative," to be (in Frank O'Hara's words) "quicker and surer than prose," and we lose patience when it isn't.[25] But this conservatism of taste (oddly reinforced during the 1960s by a lively resurgence of popular song writing) also works practically in the poet's favor. An occasional neatness of formulation or grace of cadence will keep us reading, on the chance of its happening again further along. Or we will mark passages to return to and settle for a few of them, reminding ourselves that the poetic "real thing" is never in oversupply. Such neatness and grace, in any event, remain virtues superior to ambitious outlining on however grand a scale.

This remains true even when the poet, honorably embroiled in civil crisis, declares that he or she has given up the making of poetic forms as an end in itself and will henceforth bear witness as directly as possible to a peremptory consciousness of human need. Here for example is Adrienne Rich, determined in mid-career to strip away a prize pupil's circumspection and bravely defying Auden's much-quoted formula (in the Yeats elegy) with, as John V. Morris has commented, a poetry that really intends to make something happen; a poetry, however, that has turned oddly toneless and disjunctive precisely as it reaches for an anterior moral authority. Happily it does not always lose poetic succinctness:

> I am bombarded yet   I stand
>
> I have been standing all my life in the
> direct path of a battery of signals
> the most accurately transmitted most
> untranslatable language in the universe....
>
> I am an instrument in the shape
> of a woman trying to translate pulsations
> into images   for the relief of the body
> and the reconstruction of the mind.
> "Planetarium" (1971)

Not great poetry nor even, in its voicing, fully alive to its own modest progressions, yet forthright and substantial as a statement of feeling. Is it altogether absurd to suggest that the core of what *Gravity's Rainbow* has to say of graspable importance gets expressed in these nine lines, and will not gain much in persuasiveness for all that novel's encyclopedic effort of exemplificaton?

At all events the shorter or middle-length lyric, either presented as such or enclosed within larger structures, has remained since 1950 the form most new poets have done their best work in. Modernism may have receded into history and the classroom, but its technical program still dominates current practice, if only by negation. A common schooling in the reforms and reinventions of the Pound-Williams-Stevens-Auden era, particularly as regards speech cadence and tone, comes to the surface in any review of the journals and presses where poetry goes on being published. And certainly one of the pleasures of having to do with literature at all continues to be watching out for good new work: poems, passages from poems, any casual turn or figure of verse-statement which is freshly and fittingly realized. For myself as a reader, a normal generational interest in the writing of my own nearest contemporaries has remained uncommonly rewarding. If I confined myself simply to American poets born between 1923 and 1928 I would have, to begin with, Anthony Hecht, Alan Dugan, Daniel Hoffman, Richard Hugo, Louis Simpson, Vassar Miller, Kenneth Koch, W. D. Snodgrass, A. R. Ammons, James Merrill, Robert Creeley, Allen Ginsberg, Frank O'Hara, Robert Bly, James Wright, W. S. Merwin, John Ashbery, William Dickey, Philip Levine, Irving Feldman, L. E. Sissman, to quicken expectation and redeem, a little, the slide of the times.* A residual notion of verse competence and architectonic fitness remains their common period inheritance, even though several of them have seemed tempted, at different stages in their work, to throw it all overboard.

From manifestos, prefaces, printed interviews, and from texts of the poetry itself, it would be easy to assemble evidence of a proximate revolution in

---

*Why, though, so few women of sustained accomplishment from that run of birth years, as opposed to the next five-year configuration (Rich, Sylvia Plath) or that of a decade earlier (Elizabeth Bishop, Josephine Miles, Jean Garrigue, Gwendolyn Brooks)?

poetic practice since around 1950. But it would be quite as easy to show that the revolutionizing impulse has been as incomplete, as coincidentally eager to base itself on secure precedent, as self-declared revolutions commonly are. We turn expectantly to an Allen Ginsberg for some forthright announcement of an end to inherited constrictions, and the slogans are there—never again the crabbedly "formal" and "classicist," but Whitmanesque "gab," "native wordslinging"; no more "forcing the thoughts into straightjacket," but something "as wild and as clear (really clear) as the mind[!] . . . sort of a search for the rhythm of the thoughts & their natural occurrences & spacings & notational paradigms." Or to Frank O'Hara, who, trapped for once into prose explanations, obligingly dismisses "elaborately sounded structures . . . rhythm, assonance, all that stuff," and proposes instead that "you just go on your nerve." Or to the San Franciscan Robert Duncan: not "conventions, conformities, and regulated meters," but "the exuberance of my soul"; not "taste, reason, rationality," but the swarming "chiaroscuro" of "possession," "free association." Or to Charles Olson, even more insistently theoretical and—from his perch at Black Mountain College—influential: "COMPOSITION BY FIELD, as opposed to inherited line, stanza, over-all form," with verse lines that are not deadened by "a concept of foot" but come direct "from the breathing of the man who writes."[26]

Alongside, however, in each of these pronouncements, stands some sort of reassuring appeal to established methods and principles. These newest American poet-rebels have been, if anything, *more* bookish and scholastic in argument than the Eliotized disciplinarians who allegedly barred their way to poetic fulfillment. Habitués of writing seminars and vanguard bookshops, they have been thoroughly comfortable and at home in the democratized edge-of-campus environments which since 1945 have provided most of them a base of operations. Ginsberg's recitation of influences is group doctrine—Whitman's long, emotionally shaped line; Williams's use of living talk and of blocks of direct, supposedly unprocessed observation; Hart Crane's eager trust (also attributed to Smart, Lorca, Apollinaire) in the "surreal but sensible superstructure of imagination." "Whitman and Crane and Williams" are Frank O'Hara's trinity of reliable American forerunners; somebody's obtuse dismissal of Williams is a point of departure for Duncan's meditation on "the meaning of form," which offers amplifications of Pound's teachings and a sympathetic critique of the uses and self-established limits of Marianne Moore's prosody; and it is by way of justifying a practice said to be commonplace with "sons of Pound and Williams" that Olson, benign Dutch uncle to a host of younger poets, advances his theory of "projective or OPEN verse."★

★Further, Olson, Duncan, and O'Hara all argue directly, and repeatedly, from the great formulations in Keats's letters—"negative capability," the "true voice of feeling," the importance of staying close to the mind's natural confusion ("uncertainties, mysteries, doubts")—which are the nearest thing in Anglo-American writing to a postclassical *ars poetica*.

But this particular set of preferences and admirations has not been exclusive in recent American poetry to the self-styled revolutionists. They are all but universal over the past thirty years. From the headquarters of the maligned New Criticism itself—a movement wrongly identified in recent polemic with certain drab classroom exercises in textual explication—Randall Jarrell stepped forward to celebrate the tonic "generosity and extravagance" of Williams (a poetry "more remarkable for its empathy, sympathy, its muscular and emotional identification with its subjects, than any modern poetry except Rilke's") and, even more fulsomely, the "grand ... elevated ... comprehensive ... real" poetic nerve of Walt Whitman; and it was another of Ransom's studious Kenyon brood, Robert Lowell, who would most impressively memorialize the passion and courage of Hart Crane.[27] Moreover, in no theoretical statement by Beat, Black Mountain, or Bay Area writers do we find anything more absolute, and dialectically undigested, than this declaration by the university poet A. R. Ammons, writing from his book-lined study at Cornell:

... I'm sick of good poems, all those little rondures splendidly brought off, painted gourds on a shelf: give me the dumb, debilitated, nasty, and massive, if that's the alternative: touch the universe anywhere you touch it everywhere....

Sphere, #138 (1973)

If any new poetic ethos can be said to have materialized since the 1940s, we might simply note that it did not come by way of settling the persistent critical argument between form and formlessness, or between "closed" and "open" verse. (A pseudo-argument surely: isn't all verse closed when printed, open when being written or read?) For each of the main symbolic spokesmen of this argument as it came to be waged after 1945—the somewhat patronizingly admired Williams quite as much as the shunned, and feared, Eliot—both expressive form and imaginative figuration had to have an objectifying definiteness. Different views were put on record as to how, performatively, poetic objectification was best achieved and whether personal emotion should enter directly into it or be kept at bay at all costs; but there was no disagreement about the importance of exact workmanship. That again is the universal modernist creed. Eliot's intimidating emphasis on the poet's own necessary impersonality was felt from early on to have been a deliberately contentious overstatement; and his remark years later that *The Waste Land* itself was only a piece of private rhythmical grumbling confirmed impressions that he too had been using poetry (and criticism) as a cathartic defense of endangered personality, beginning with his own.

The very terms of that presumptive debate have come to seem inconsequential, as if no longer germane to actual poetic choice. When all personal being and the natural universe as well are felt to be threatened by vast conspiracies of degradation, any view of poetic practice which is not focused on the defense of primary resources comes under an equal suspicion. One theory of technical perfection is as irrelevant as another to the writer's overmastering concern with staying alive as writer. (I am not saying that this is as it should be; I am saying that this is how it has been.) The "rhythm" and "flow" of unmediated feeling; the fight to maintain enough "nerve" to stay in the game at all; the protection of the soul's primal reserve of "exuberance"; the animal "breathing" that is the last warrant of creaturely life—all these (in the diction of the 1950–1961 texts cited above) not only appear as actions of mind infinitely more precious than the art that would encapsulate them but seem actively threatened by that art's expressive requirements. The odd thing is, of course, that since these are all essentially biological qualities, properties of animate life wherever found, their realization in sequences of words and verses might as well be anonymous and unindividualized, without effective distinction of form. The famous theory of poetic impersonality no longer needs to be argued, the thing itself having descended on poetic utterance like a long shriveling drought.

The result in the years following 1950 is a poetry that in its actual progressions seems more and more fearful of getting ensnared in any conclusive realization. (This ambivalence became one of Stevens's last subjects: the terror, expressed in certain short poems of the early 1950s, of thought's sealing itself off at last within a figured emptiness of its own making, without answering resemblance; the correlative terror of some independent "x" or "region November" or "bronze decor" rising "beyond the last thought.")

The flight from traditional forms becomes a flight, too, from the concentrating imaginative passion which in earlier Romantic theory was the ultimate guarantee of both formal fitness and emotional spontaneity.* What is feared now, we can say, is contingent experience itself. It is as if any and every sentient occurrence exposed the mind to control systems as potentially destructive of selfhood as the vast institutional conspiracies dreamed up by novelists. The very act of writing, as it wholly absorbs the attention of the mind it issues from, comes under suspicion; only an autotechnic of "nerve" and "breath" can really be trusted. The whole two-fold contingency of poetic making becomes the ultimate entrapment: its dependence on an influx of feeling or vision from sources not strictly identical with itself; its corresponding subjection to self-contained language structures which the poet in his own person cannot have originated and cannot hope to regulate in the damaged consciousness of his auditors. For the

---

*A theory and a faith the self-styled Beats did steadfastly hold to. Allen Ginsberg's first explanations of what he was attempting have the character of a good student's lucid synthesis of favorite lessons. To Richard Eberhart he defended "Howl" in 1956 as an "expression of natural ecstasy," a release of "my own heart's instincts" and "true feelings"—which is Keats again: "I am certain of nothing but of the holiness of the Heart's affections and the truth of Imagination." Yet he also described the poem as gaining its effects through a careful observance of rules of design appropriate to the expressive "experiment" it represented. Eberhart was urged not to mistake "Howl" in this respect: "The poem is really built like a brick shithouse." See *To Eberhart from Ginsberg* (Lincoln, Massachusetts: Penmaen Press, 1976), pp. 17–31.

poet, then, what practical choice is left but one or another strategy of withdrawal and dissociation, even from his own hard-won competence as poet?

Is there clear evidence that something like this is in fact the case with the poetry now being written—or has been perceived as the case by those most concerned? That such evidence is not only abundant but comes in a form already organized for literary-historical assessment is itself both paradox and sign of the times. Uncertainties about the legitimacy of the whole process and economy of the poetic act steadily increase, but so does the sheer mass of new poems and books of poems. Established poets publish more frequently now in their sixth and seventh decades of life than they did at thirty or forty, and interesting new ones come forward in all the appropriate motions of the well-launched career. It was in fact to deal with both these circumstances, the epidemic uncertainty and the runaway increase of individual instances, that several new journals devoted entirely to reviewing current work, like *Parnassus* and *Poetry Now*, were established early in the 1970s. Assigning reviews for the most part to other working poets, such journals were conceived as providing a more orderly and knowledgeable clinic, so to speak, where the community of poetry might regularly monitor its own vital signs.

And for the moment it is this professional community's self-assessment rather than my own budget of impressions that I am interested in recording. What follows is a summary of the critical testimony rendered in the first two years' run of the journal *Parnassus* (founded in 1972); an account, that is, of what American poetry now amounts to, thirty years into "postmodernism," in the judgment of those who most diligently keep track of it and who also, much of the time, are actively occupied with writing it.

Their testimony does indeed form a consensus, and it is fairly overwhelming. What is described and scrupulously illustrated on all sides is a shrinkage of the imaginative field of poetic statement to the contemplative and merely reactive, or abreactive, self—not the self which has its place within a continuum of vital relationship but a self which seems more and more deprived of assurance as to its basic purchase on active life, more and more unwilling to act in turn as a corresponsive agent and force. The myth of power and creative efficacy implicit in the very words *poetry* and *poem* begins to seem a hollow joke. (Myths *can* die, anthropologists remind us.) To maintain itself in at least a semblance of its remembered functions, poetic utterance withdraws into exercises of self-preservation. No more the egotistical sublime of high Romanticism, early or late, but egotism terrorized and turned spectral, or—where there are still currents of poetic energy in the remembered sense—turned self-parodic and self-consuming.

It should be said, too, that what is being described in this reviewers' consensus is not merely a wholesale convergence on the aptly named confessional mode which materialized during the later

1950s with Allen Ginsberg and friends and with *Heart's Needle* and *Life Studies* (both 1959). Yet some comparable contraction appears universal. A calculated retreat in mid-career from poems of general wisdom and truth, formally self-verifying, into private recollection and a backward-looking self-communion is now seen as common to nearly all of Lowell's poetic generation (as suggested above, chapter two). Eventually it would produce, in *The Dream Songs* and sections of *History*, the most liberally entertaining poetry in English of the past quarter century. (What modern work stands nearer the great precedent of Milton's sonnets to contemporary artists, friends, and public heroes than Berryman's and Lowell's poems commemorating the worthies of their own age and calling?) But among the crowd of younger, later-arriving poets this retreat no longer seems to represent a reasoned choice. Here, for instance, is Jascha Kessler's comment in an omnibus review: "Like [poet A] and like [poet B], too, [poet C] is confined to Selfdom, if not Selfhood," while poet D, equally confined, "seems to be forcing himself to write poems," as if for want of other acceptable work.* Some of what results is sympathetically allowed the secondary value of social documentation. At the least it brings hard news of other people's lives: not the greatest service literature

---

*Where the critical comment is altogether dismissive, nothing is served by attaching names. Those maliciously interested may consult *Parnassus*, vols. I–II (1972–1974), where all reviews are conveniently identified in the table of contents by both author and subject.

might perform but one we probably cannot have too much of. "Lucille Clifton," according to her appreciative reviewer, "writes about what it means to be a black woman who grew up in the 1940's"; and Helen Vendler, surveying Adrienne Rich's whole career, recalls her own "disbelieving wonder" at discovering in the early 1950s that "someone my age was writing down my life." A "documentary record," is Eric Mottram's summary of a new collection by Denise Levertov; not, finally, a "memorable" record, yet one with genuine evidentiary value.

But more decisively a contraction or attenuation even within the personal mode is widely reported. In most of these poems the unattached, unrelated self is felt to be standing warily apart even from its own registered experience. ("An endless autobiography," Eric Mottram, again, writes of a volume by Diane Wakoski, but one burdened with "a passionately alert sense of the *uselessness* of self-regard.") The self may yearn for a relation that will be simple (i.e., direct), and sensuous, and passionate—Milton's three properties of high poetic achievement—and will perhaps reach out for such a relation or the nourishing recollection of it. But it is seen as reaching from a disabling separateness and distance. One sees the affective point of one of Ammons's typically indistinct and toneless ruminations in his "Essay on Poetics" [sic]: "Strings of nucleations please me more than representative details."[28] Apparently the judgment of what is "representative" requires more assurance about one's standpoint of judgment and one's grasp on the things to be judged than the self who writes can any longer muster.

For all its insistent subjectivity the poetry under review seems to its readers remote and emotionally empty. Its real ground of interest corresponds to what Blanche Gelfant has shrewdly identified as the ground of interest and appeal in the shapeless mass of Jack Kerouac's prose: the sense of "helplessness" it conveys, and of the writer's having been wholly "depleted" by the experience his work represents.[29] What success such poetry does achieve is said to depend in any case on the existence of a specially trained and prepared readership, since much of the time (according to the reviewer of some Black Mountain verse) the constitutive perceptions and ideas "barely manage to reach the page." "A good book," Paul Zweig writes of William Dickey, "finely tuned to complicated emotions; lit up every so often by moments of ... generous insight. Yet the poems seem to happen far away," as if able to take shape only at a blurring distance. Or John Bayley on W. S. Merwin: "The poetry of a kind of inner cultivation, requiring an audience with something of the same degree of experience and refinement, with expectations and preknowledge of what is going on." Not a bad thing at all, one would add—and as Louis Simpson remarked on a similar occasion, "It is hardly the poet's fault that there are few readers for this kind of poetry"[30]—but a precariously limited and self-insulating basis for fresh invention. "Outside the classroom," Paul Mariani asks, "how many others *read* [these] poems?"

What is also crushingly reported by the *Parnassus* consensus is a simultaneous attenuation of poetic form and language. The favored compositional form appears to be the private journal, a solution which circumvents the more demanding problems of compositional order yet still can aspire to the weight and authority of extended statement. It is in the "respectable tradition of the verse-journal" that William Meredith places Ammons's later writing, from *Tape* to *Sphere*. Helen Vendler sees that this is what the uneven mass of Frank O'Hara's poetry composes; its "generic form . . . is conversation, the *journal intime*." Ginsberg has been explicit, in his own case, on the point of form: "Not exactly poems, nor not poems: journal notations put together conveniently."[31] And Berryman, too, in the poem "Message" midway through *Love & Fame* (1970), as if needing to lay to rest once more the specter of *The Prelude*: "I am not writing an autobiography-in-verse, my friends"—nothing, that is, with the "amplitude" and "voltage" you ask me for—but fragments only:

> Impressions, structures, tales from Columbia
>   in the Thirties
> & the Michaelmas term at Cambridge in '36,
> followed by some later, It's not my life.

But so, too, Donald Davie, in *Parnassus*, on all of Lowell since *Life Studies*: his poems are "skimmed off . . . life," Davie remarks, and have in themselves "no more [poetic] direction than entries in a journal." Lowell's work in this vein, sections of which have appeared less discordantly in the politically conversant *New York Review of Books* than almost any other poet's verse (in English), reminds us that there can be such a thing as a public journal, too: the day-by-day life record of a man who, like the audience he writes for, reads the newspapers, fitfully watches television, meditates on his own bad faith, and keeps anguished account of an onslaught of events he feels powerless to affect or even come into intelligible relation with. (It is a strategy which is both strength and limitation in Lowell's most ambitious poem of the *Life Studies* interval, "For the Union Dead.") Lowell himself, in his revised "Afterthought" to *Notebook* (1970), debated whether the work should be read as "an almanac" or as "the story of my life." (In the first printing of *Notebook* he had specifically denied that it was either one.) Is there any longer much difference?

If the journal or journalized autobiographical fragment is our reigning formal solution, it has also become very possibly our chief instrument of performative self-deception. Each of the foregoing examples can be substantively challenged by a broad caveat the German critic Walter Benjamin issued half a century ago against the too immediate serviceability of the journal as a literary form. "The danger," he wrote, "is always in laying bare, in the soul, the germs of remembrance much sooner than artistically they should be, and in preventing the maturing of their fruits."* Imagination in the verse-journal risks

---

*The comment comes in a discussion of Goethe's use of an aphoristic journal in the novel, *Elective Affinities*, to establish themes and perceptions eluding clear narrative definition. What equally catches attention now is Benjamin's unwavering 1920s confidence in the power of fully composed art, against all odds,

yielding too easily to fragmentation and linear stockpiling. Each entry needs only to fill the space on the page that the calendar reserves for it.

For poetry this danger materializes most immediately in language, verse idiom. Here is where the spreading indifference to concentration and resolution seems most extreme. To judge by the *Parnassus* reviewers, all our media-age fears and alarms about some radical atrophy in language capacity have not come a day too soon. A chief practical truth about our recent poetry appears to be that almost nobody hesitates to write it or—worse—print it as soon as written. Helen Vendler, in a *New York Times* roundup, was moved to this general characterization of half a year's new work: "Too often simply garrulous, self-indulgent and self-absorbed, written in a hurry, eager for instant effect."[32] "Hysteria seems to be our muse," Theodore Weiss remarks, "the only goddess we believe in." Yet to Weiss (whose taste and practiced judgment span the whole era considered in this book) the most curious aspect of so much self-absorption and personalization is the fundamental monotony of what results, the sameness in the speaking voice. I do still exist, wanly or frantically these poems contrive to tell us, but only as I shed the responsibility of identifying anything precisely, of marking clear distinctions between contingent things, even of leaving a traceable voiceprint of my own. Edwin Fussell—reporting, it is true, from

---

to bring imaginative apprehension to full term. See Walter Benjamin, *Goethes Wahlverwandtschaften* (Frankfurt: Insel-Verlag, 1955), p. 76.

California, where every fearful dream finds its confirming image roaring down the freeway; yet reporting on new books by two widely published and respected poets—simply threw up his hands in terminal dismay: "Literary historians of the future may well rack up 1973 as the year in which the American language disappeared."

By common report the chief exception to these bleak judgments, and the cleanest verse now being written, comes in a poetry carefully limited to descriptions of natural objects and processes. It keeps, that is, to materials which have the immense initial advantage of being free from the normal complications of human exchange. In the flight from a world in which every asserted relationship seems irreversibly compromising, this mode—which for all local differences oddly resembles a new, recessive Georgianism—strongly attracts poets who are in search of some altogether different pattern of everyday existence, as well as those grandchildren of Pound's schoolbook formula of 1917 about "the man who wants to do a good job." ("Man" seems appropriate here; nowadays women poets seem less inclined to settle for daydreams of some untainted otherness of being.) Predictably Gary Snyder, endlessly journeying toward a deeper concord with physical life, has taken the mode to extremes, in monotone extensions of the Pacific Coast naturalism Robinson Jeffers brought into poetry in the 1920s. Snyder indeed has wanted to make this solution prescriptive for poetry in general. As title for one of his poems in *Regarding Wave* (1970) he sets the question,

"What you should know to be a Poet," and gives as his principal answer:

> all you can about animals as persons
> the names of trees and flowers and weeds
> names of stars, and the movement of the planets
>   and the moon

—nothing, that is, in this purgative nominalism, which might pull you back into the disturbances of human association (animals and persons having become interchangeable); and then, as to technique, no suggestion that it would help to know something about the energies of verbs, about forms of syntax other than the paratactic and appositional, or about the kind of figuration even fetishes need in order to exert a positive charm.*

    A. R. Ammons, however, trusting to his "strings of nucleations," would suggest that this kind of recitative detachment supplies all the figuration needed. "The designs are there," the "Essay on Poetics" explains: "I use words to draw them out." The verb *use* seems just right for the gnostic simplifications this rests on. (Is it perverse to hear in it a flattening tonality from one's own misspent Sunday School youth, when visiting killjoys would talk about "using" or "not using" liquor and tobacco?) Yet isn't it the economy of extractive "using" that we once thought the arts might rescue us from?

---

*Is this unjust? Later in the poem Snyder writes: "& then love the human: wives husbands and friends." Even here, though, the undifferentiated generality of the list appears modeled on zoonomic classification.

In this crisis not only for the language of poetry but for the very "way of happening" (Auden again, in the Yeats elegy) that makes it poetry, what outgoing vitality is still to be found in poetic speech seems concentrated in parody and self-mockery. By such means a crippling doubt about the legitimacy of being a poet at all, let alone choosing any one definite voice to speak in—anxieties both duly noted by *Parnassus* reviewers—can at least find relief in a mimicking playfulness. If poetry can't lick the etiolations besetting it, it can at least join them; it can try to beguile the demon of inauthenticity back onto terrain already occupied. To my ear this deviation into parody and self-parody is the main instrument of much that seems most durable in the period as a whole. Certainly it is what most frequently brings poetic animation into Ginsberg's and O'Hara's self-communings, plugging them into an actual world of life-burdened speech and common vernacular complicity. At a further reach of self-concentration the same deviation antiphonally sustains the arguments of opposing voices and selves with which Berryman, in the elegiac *Dream Songs*, outwits the death-fear he was condemned to harbor as his muse; as it was a primary means by which Sylvia Plath, best when wittiest, forced her destructive genius to yield up its extraordinary poetic blessing.

What is also more than routinely curious is that this reported deterioration in verse language has coincided with the institutionalization of the public reading as the central medium of our poetry's continuing existence. Such readings, where poems that rarely circulate enough to meet printing costs are listened to by audiences who will not have read very much but are more than ready to be startled into some primitive return of faith, seem more and more the determining occasion for which poetry goes on being written. And it may be that writing that reviewers reasonably characterize as garrulous, monotonous, word-careless and the like, has simply been misunderstood in its primary function—which is to furnish disposable scripts the poet can use in acting out his fiction of personal consequence, in the validating presence of an audience very much like himself and not less hungry for some bluff gesture of self-authentication.

These readings have the character of a privileged by-ritual, and they serve, we can agree, a decent civil purpose. It is as if for the space of an hour a company of survivors had come together in retreat to hear one of its members testify how, currently, it is with him (Emerson's American prescription for what all poetry should convey); how therefore it might also be with them. Anyone who has gone to a reading by Gary Snyder and followed his gentle lead in creating an atmosphere where everything that exists is welcomed to the table (as in some latter-day perfectionist conventicle) forgets all about the inertness of words on pages. So also with a reading by Robert Creeley: the sometimes nearly strangling effort to strike all inauthenticity or presumption from each phrase as it emerges makes criticism seem as inappropriate as at any ongoing birth trauma. And what one remembers, thinking back to one of Anne

Sexton's desperately skillful public performances, is how that harsh linear shuttle of self-humiliation and aggressive self-recovery could be as compelling to live audiences as an expert singer's delivery of a set of banal song texts. From readings by the black poets Etheridge Knight and Ishmael Reed, too, it is the shared atmosphere of the whole occasion that stays in mind, along with the poet's personal resilience in dealing with the mortifications of black life: warm humor and bitter friendliness in the one instance, a sly aggressive-submissive mockery in the other, with the phrased detail of each manner rooted (like Ellison's prose) in recognizable formulas of vernacular resistance.*

See how it is, just now, that I survive, runs the reading poet's message. So we too might survive, is the coherent sense his audience makes of it. And perhaps it is, in a word, a survivor's poetry we have to content ourselves with at present. ("A way to survive with others," is Diane Middlebrook's comment in *Parnassus* on a new installment of Allen Ginsberg's verse notebook.) All through the modernist era, literature, like disciplined thought and art in

---

*Another concise remark of Walter Benjamin's is to the point here: that the whole "historical situation of contemporary literature" is becoming one in which old distinctions between author and public are vanishing away ("The Work of Art in the Age of Mechanical Reproduction," *Illuminations,* trans. Harry Zohn [New York: Harcourt, Brace and World, 1968], pp. 233–234). Poetry primarily shaped by the anticipation of public readings exists as poetry only through the physical participation of an audience that in turn increasingly imposes its own limiting conditions of acceptance.

general, continued to be energized by a shared confidence in the writer's fundamental power over everything contingent. It was a power to transcend confusion; to bring equilibrium out of conflict; to reconcile those contradictions which are paralyzing or worse; to restore balance, remedy deprivation, reverse entropy, substitute protocols of concord and relation for evolutionary turbulence; to give freely, and sympathize, and control; to demonstrate the immediate sensible reality of love and freedom or their terrible opposites; and in all these ways to augment a human future still conceived as potentially open and reparative. Now, instead, writing is produced which is by, and for, and mostly about survivors—persons living on after the decisive things have happened—as if no one could remember any other condition of being.

Like any sanctioned convention such writing has its own ways of turning corrupt, as with what Helen Vendler, a leading corruption spotter, has spoken of as the awful "spunkiness" of the self-approving "survival artist."[33] But at its level best it furnishes speech ceremonies we reasonably cling to and hope to have repeated—for it testifies that our unnerving apprehensiveness is no mere private affliction; that our hours of fear are not unshared and their objects are indeed in some respects as we obscurely perceive them. The virtue such writing recovers may only be the minimum virtue of temporal appropriateness; literally, a marking of time and of the times. But without that minimum the practice of poetry, and of criticism too, would make no acceptable claim at all on our continuing attention.

Bearing Witness, Negotiating Survival

Surprisingly, though, for all that the foregoing may have of historical truth about it, our poets have not failed from time to time to present such claims, and continue to reach us with them, overcoming every distraction, every interference, our era can contrive. It wouldn't be fair, at the end of this all too rebarbative account, not to let a few of them speak briefly for themselves:

> Days: And think
> of all those cluttered instruments,
> one to a fact,
> canceling each other's experience;
> how they were
> like some hideous calendar
> "Compliments of Never & Forever, Inc."
> Elizabeth Bishop, "Argument" (1955)

As usual in New York, everything is torn down
Before you have had time to care for it.
Head bowed, at the shrine of noise, let me try to recall
What building stood here. Was there a building at all?
I have lived on this same street for a decade.
James Merrill, "An Urban Convalescence" (1962)

... I walk up the muggy street beginning to sun
and have a hamburger and a malted and buy
an ugly NEW WORLD WRITING to see what the poets
in Ghana are doing these days. . . .

. . . then I go back where I came from to 6th Avenue
and the tobacconist in the Ziegfield Theatre and
casually ask for a carton of Gauloises and a carton
of Picayunes, and a NEW YORK POST with her face on it

and I am sweating a lot by now and thinking of
leaning on the john door in the 5 SPOT

while she whispered a song along the keyboard
to Mal Waldron and everyone and I stopped breathing
> Frank O'Hara, "The Day Lady Died" (1964)

I am incapable of more knowledge.
What is this, this face
So murderous in its strangle of branches?—

Its snaky acids kiss.
It petrifies the will. These are the isolate, slow faults
That kill, that kill, that kill.
> Sylvia Plath, "Elm" (1962)*

America you don't really want to go to war.
America it's them bad Russians.
Them Russians them Russians and them Chinamen. And them Russians.
The Russia wants to eat us alive. The Russia's power mad. She wants to take our cars from out our garages.
Her wants to grab Chicago. Her needs a Red Reader's Digest. Her wants our auto plants in Siberia. Him big bureaucracy running our fillingstations.
That no good. Ugh. Him make Indians learn read. Him need big black niggers. Hah. Her make us all work sixteen hours a day. Help.
America this is quite serious.
> Allen Ginsberg, "America" (1956)

"In that
future American Era I shall enter a new form: to cure
the world of loveless knowledge that seeks with blind hunger;
and mindless rage eating food that will not fill it."

---

*Not the least of this poem's merits is that it closes, in these lines, with the only successful borrowing of Emily Dickinson's short-meter stanza I know of in twentieth-century poetry.

And he showed himself in his true form of
SMOKEY THE BEAR

A handsome smokey-colored brown bear standing on his hind legs, showing that he is aroused and watchful.

Bearing in his right paw the Shovel that digs to the truth beneath appearance; cuts the roots of useless attachments, and flings damp sand on the fires of greed and war . . .

        Gary Snyder, "Smokey the Bear Sutra" (1960s?)

. . . desperate to devise anything, any
sadness or happiness, only
to escape the clasped coffinworm
truth of eternal art or marmoreal

infinite nature, twin stiff
destined measures both manifested
by my shoes, coated with dust or dew which no
earthly measure will survive.
    Robert Pinsky, "Sadness and Happiness" (1975)

    . . . Look at
what passes for the new.

You will not find it there but in
    despised poems.
      It is difficult

to get the news from poems
    yet men die miserably every day
      for lack

Of what is found there.
        William Carlos Williams,
           "Asphodel" (1955)

4

Old Masters: Henry Miller and Wallace Stevens

> How the hell can a man write when he doesn't know where he's going to sit the next half-hour?
>
> **Henry Miller,** *Tropic of Cancer* (1934)

> From this the poem springs: that we live in a place
> That is not our own. . . .
>
> **Wallace Stevens,**
> "Notes Toward a Supreme Fiction" (1942)

Opulent or barren, a new literary-historical period can both surprise us with its abrupt changes (or cessations) and yet oblige us to acknowledge that with a finer attentiveness we might have seen the like of it coming. In this fashion a sudden increase of masterly new works and original signatures will challenge critical awareness to major readjustments of working principle—as the trajectory of high modernism eventually set off more than one new-critical revolt. But so also will a protracted lull in authentic creativity. That, too, is a provocation challenging every expectation and assurance. At the least, as it disconcertingly persists, it nourishes suspicions that there may well have occurred some substantial loss or abridgment of the collaborative readiness any richly satisfying art will be found to have risen from. In time we find reasons why the new condition of things has come about, and eventually we piece together a scenario of how it took hold. And in the process certain irregular events at the threshold of the transformation in question begin to look different to us. They seem now to stand much nearer than was originally suspected to the new period's distinctive unfolding, so that it, too, as a collective development, proves to have had the same kind of positive "foreground" which Emerson imagined for the single new work or voice of incontestable authority.

The foreground to be reviewed in this chapter comprises the writing of two notably independent figures who were in their creative prime in the years leading into the 1945–1975 era and who, looked back on from the latter end of it, more and more seem to me to have anticipated with particular clarity its central imaginative character. Casting them in such a role or indeed bringing them together for any serious critical purpose may have, at a glance, little to recommend it. Admittedly, if we were to set about reconstructing the literary milieu just before and during the Second World War, Henry Miller and Wallace Stevens would probably not be the first names to come to mind. Yet neither can be described as suffering indifference and neglect during those years, nor as lacking, by 1945, a substantial critical reputation. Miller, in his middle fifties, was already a scandal of censorship on two continents and the main figure of reference in a suitably apocalyptic essay by George Orwell, then at the height of *his* powers, prophesying the imminent breakup of the whole laissez-faire capitalist, liberal-Christian order. And Stevens was, at sixty-six, ten years forward in that extraordinary resurgence of poetic energy which, having lately brought him through the composition of two long, ambitious meditative poems ("Notes Toward a Supreme Fiction," "Esthétique du Mal"), had for the moment all but displaced his best-known American contemporaries in the attention of the bellwether literary journals.[1]

But I am not concerned here to nominate Miller and Stevens as the foremost American writers of the 1930–1945 interval, though there are readers of impressive critical passion who have done just that.* The Nobel laurels that went in succession to Eliot and Faulkner at the end of the 1940s were not, I think, misdelivered. Neither am I offering Miller and Stevens as the chief practical models for important new writing in the United States through the 1950s, 1960s, and 1970s; though once you begin to look, evidence multiplies of their having been more concretely influential—Miller especially—than we are yet fully aware (see Coda). On the other hand, in no way do I mean to suggest that the interest of their

---

*Introducing the first legal edition of *Tropic of Cancer* in 1961, Karl Shapiro described Miller as, simply, our greatest living author. Professor Harold Bloom, in numerous essays, has urged on us an estimate of Stevens that "sets him higher than Frost, Pound, Eliot, or Williams" (*Figures of Capable Imagination* [New York: Seabury Press, 1976], p. 103), and now in a long eloquent book claims for his final twenty years "a glory almost unique in the poetry of the last several centuries" (*Wallace Stevens* [Ithaca: Cornell University Press, 1977], p. 89).

writing is now mainly historical and anticipatory. Quite the contrary: to return to Miller and Stevens across the literary epoch that has intervened is to feel as acutely as ever the vitality and self-sufficiency each acquired along his own creative path. They merely seem to me, now, the two American writers who at the beginning of our period had already assimilated into their working character the themes, attitudes, and expressive intentionalities I have so far itemized in this book.

2

Henry Miller is something more than a one-book author—his evocations of exotic human environments like the Greece of *The Colossus of Maroussi* or the Brooklyn remembered in *Black Spring* and elsewhere remain impressionistically lively and convincing—but what he mainly counts for in literary history is fully displayed in his first and most organized book, *Tropic of Cancer* (1934). Orwell accurately remarked of it that the date of publication is somewhat misleading. The "mental atmosphere" of the book, he pointed out, really belongs to the 1920s rather than the 1930s; most precisely, to that end-of-the-twenties moment when the modernist impulsion that had made Paris its world capital seemed rapidly fraying out into imitation and self-parody and all of Europe had begun to sense the onset of catastrophes more appalling than those of 1914–1918.[2]

Tropic of Cancer, Orwell continued, sees this historical moment clearly enough, more clearly indeed than most of those whose concern was to master it by rigorous ideological analysis and either ride the wave of it or offer effective resistance. But what is remarkable to Orwell, and much more disturbing than the book's forthright plunge into obscenity and squalor, is that the author has washed his hands of any shred of personal responsibility. Nothing in the world is more absurd to him than the illusion that individual men and women have anything to gain by staking their existence, their chance of happiness, on world-historical developments: "He believes in the impending ruin of Western Civilization much more firmly than the majority of 'revolutionary' writers; only he does not feel called upon to do anything about it."[3]

The flat judgment Orwell finishes with, that Miller is "a completely negative, unreconstructive, amoral writer," considerably simplifies his actual findings, and is contradicted in any case by his perception of the twenties ambiance of Miller's writing. In its two great dithyrambic climaxes *Tropic of Cancer* celebrates, in twenties fashion, the visionary power of two artists, Matisse and Joyce, from the same ranks of master painters and writers that furnished Proust his ideal types of heroic virtue. But they are magnificent, in Miller's descriptions, only by way of a conspicuous anachronism. The beauty Matisse has created exists in serene disregard of the mass degradations of contemporary life; it is beautiful "in an old-fashioned bedroom way," evoking that idyllic premechanized world, natural and complete, "that went gaily to the Bois in the pastoral days of wine and fornication" (149);* while Joyce, "the great blind Milton of our times," has countered the despair of modern life by musically recreating a world in which the flowing plenitude of night and natural time has recovered its original dominion (232–233).[4]

Yet even if we do accept conventional views of the literary epoch of the 1930s and see it as centrally defined by political and ideological choice, *Tropic of Cancer* will not seem out of phase historically. It too is a novel with a purpose. The book is in fact as insistently ideological in its premises as any novel of the decade, and far more steadily so than the sentimentalized civil parables of an American contemporary like Steinbeck. The political ideology it comes nearest to endorsing is anarchism, but what is radical about *Tropic of Cancer* runs deeper than that. The true anarchist would replace imposed political obligations with the collaborative loyalty of established work groups and with territorial or regional bondings, and he would base public order on spontaneous as opposed to statutory law. Anarchism is still a politics, and a voluntary communalism is its ideal civil fulfillment. But Miller instinctively separates himself, as he can materially afford to, from human crowding of any kind. For him as for Poe and Baudelaire a century earlier, a "man of the crowd" like the frantic womanizer Van Norden—

*Here and in all subsequent citations of the text of *Tropic of Cancer*, parenthetical page references are to the Grove Press paperback edition (1961).

whose "one fear is to be left alone" (117)—epitomizes all modern insanity; and if he himself chooses to live in the mechanized hell of Paris, that is simply because day by day it is easier there than elsewhere to cadge meals or sleeping quarters and keep himself from getting bored. He would in any case reject a law based on communal will or on work-group identity as resolutely as a law descending from Mt. Sinai in the form of ten incontrovertible commandments. His ideology is rather the classic American counterposition of antinomianism, that intoxicating faith which begins by rejecting all accredited systems and formulas as conspiracies to sell you out body and soul, and which proclaims instead the end of ideology and the need before anything else to immerse yourself (as man, as writer) directly in the flow of life, wherever it carries you.

As Orwell acknowledged, it is a position that does not necessarily destroy political understanding. To Miller at the beginning of the 1930s, writing in advance of the Moscow trials (and before the Nazi accession in Germany), politics is a choice between Soviet communism and American capitalism. But on the basis of their proponents' rhetoric these supposed alternatives sound pretty much the same to him: societal systems with equally unnatural designs on their citizenry (Prohibition, the Five-Year Plan) and far too much of the organized bureaucratic power and utopian earnestness essential to enforcing those designs. Miller's antipolitical naturalism is tactically unqualified. And unlike the naturalism of Dreiser or

Hemingway or even that music of a purely natural order which in "The Man with the Blue Guitar" (1937) Stevens provisionally invokes to "take the place / Of empty heaven and its hymns," it is without ulterior personal motive. That is, Miller expects no personal advantage from it. Yet he is undisturbed by the contrary possibility of its miring him in a disorder and incapacity as destructive as the human-historical contaminations he is trying to shake off. His outlook is not amoral—what elected attitude is?—but it is shockingly free of personal anxiety; it affords no built-in escape hatch for crisis conditions, no self-exempting reserve clause against historical nightmare.

And to Miller it offers the imaginative satisfactions of being best adapted to things as they are. Or as, in the everyday world, they are palpably coming to be. For my chief point about Henry Miller is simply that everything essential to the dominating vision of life recorded by American fiction after 1945 and particularly in the 1960s and 1970s—the apparent withdrawal of any life-serving purpose from normative human relationships; the transformation of the whole institutionalized world into either an absurd farce or an openly murderous global conspiracy—is accepted as already given in *Tropic of Cancer*. Even that horrific revelation of tailgunner Snowden's "secret" toward which (not without genuine skill in the narrative design) *Catch-22* drags itself along, the revelation that "man was matter," entrails that spill out like soup, garbage that in the end merely rots or burns, would be to Miller the commonest of self-evident truths.* It is the recognition his book starts from.

Paranoia, too, cuts a broad swath through his Gallo-American milieu, but Miller himself is fairly free of it. (When he writes, "they are trying to get rid of me" [25], he simply means that two acquaintances determined to have it out with each other want him to camp for a while in some other apartment.) Mostly, paranoia is a phenomenon he observes in others, and warily pulls back from. But this is not because he harbors any saving optimism about his own or anybody's chances for survival. That the historical world is a "mad slaughterhouse" (164), a "cancer eating itself away" (2), a disintegrating wheel rolling downhill and keeping only the rush of its descent intact (148–150); that the production of suicidal poisons and explosives is its determining business (240–241); that "a new ice age is setting in" (148); that "the future belongs to the machine, to the robots" (217); that the world is becoming "a gray desert" (240); that humanity itself is being solidified into a mass of creaking machinery, enslaved to death-dealing creeds and principles (229): all this, Miller would say, must be self-evident to anyone who not only remembers the plain facts of 1914–1918 (allusions to which abound in the text) but also

*The exasperated reply that in the second chapter of *Catch-22* Clevinger makes to Yossarian (they're trying to kill *everyone*, not just you) would be Miller's reply, too, if we take away Clevinger's near-apoplexy in delivering it. To see the matter as universal does make a difference, though Yossarian never understands why.

understands that the peacetime world is merely a continuation of 1914–1918 by other means.

These vast prophetic images, however, somewhat misrepresent the main tonality of Miller's book and the state of mind it expresses. *Tropic of Cancer* is, all things considered, a cheerful and extroverted affair as it swaggers along. One agrees with Orwell: it is the book "of a man who is happy," who on the whole is enjoying himself as he lives and writes.*[5] The book's affability in the presence of its materials and themes seems genuine enough, and I think continues to seem so on a re-reading. It knows what it is looking at and is not paralyzed or even much surprised, though now and then it expresses a reassuring puzzlement at the strange power of human absurdity or misery to persist in its own path. (Only in

---

*Enjoying himself to the point of not noticing or caring when, even by his own free standards, he is writing sloppily. *Tropic of Cancer* is by no means formless, even though in the American tradition of literary rebellion it ostensibly jettisons the mystique of form and style and aims at exemplifying instead "the triumph of the individual over art" (10). Nor is it simply unprocessed talk, as Orwell contended in emphasizing its inferiority to *Ulysses*. But it does have its share of those windy and diffuse runs of "native wordslinging" (to borrow Allen Ginsberg's Milleresque phrase) which became the norm in too much of Miller's later work; those cadenzas of a kind of automatic writing unanchored in concrete observation and based instead on tags and echoes from his voluminous reading—for like most who propose to transcribe without mediation that elemental experience which is said to have been omitted from standard literature (10), he is incorrigibly bookish as a writer. More than one of his monologues develops as a mosaic of familiar quotations. But one learns, with Miller, to see such passages coming and turn the pages even faster.

the elusive undertheme of Miller's separation from his wife Mona—she lingering in "cold, glittering, malign" New York, the "white prison" [61]; he footloose in "a Paris that has never existed except by virtue of my loneliness, my hunger for her" [160-162]—does *Tropic of Cancer* expose unresolved obsession.)

One would be mistaken also to take Miller at his word that the solution to life, the way out of misery and fear, is simply "to read the zodiac and study your entrails" (220). This is not in fact how he shows himself living, nor is it how he writes. One difference between *Tropic of Cancer* and various ambitious books of the post-1945 period which are comparably autobiographical—proper novels like *The Catcher in the Rye, The Adventures of Augie March, An American Dream*; private histories like Frank Conroy's *Stop-Time*, James McConkey's *Crossroads*, Robert M. Pirsig's *Zen and the Art of Motorcycle Maintenance*—is that Miller continuously fills out, and in abundance, a world of actual persons and relationships which is not primarily a projection of his own willed purchase on life. His book is engagingly full of other people, a thing rare enough in our solipsizing literature to deserve comment. It considerably qualifies his own self-explanatory citation, in the book's epigraph, of Emerson's call for a literature of "diaries and autobiographies" instead of "novels"; qualifies also the implications of the Poe-derived challenge to lay bare "all that is in his heart" (224). Most of the time the business at hand is simply "to see and hear things" (260), to get at "what it was all about" when somebody else's obsession takes the stage (152), to be "all eyes and ears" for any new story or passing adventure that for the moment "took me completely out of myself" (178). Only the required reference to negative capability seems missing from this checklist of post-1950 performative values.

Even within *Cancer*'s self-limited society of drifters, crackpots, neurasthenics, climbers, spongers, parasites, and whores, a sizeable gallery of contemporary portraits emerges; a biographical mini-dictionary sufficiently differentiated to have the feeling of general or collective truth. Van Norden is not Carl, Collins is not Fillmore, Tania is by no stretch of the imagination identical with Germaine or Elsa or Macha or Ginette; Moldorf, Kruger, and Mark Swift are possessed by measurably different demons (though the first two are American Jews); and each one of the floating subcommunity of international exiles appears devious and self-deluding in his or her own way. Most important, these figures as displayed in the text all acquire what is essential to fictive acceptance, and that is the capacity to occupy real narrative space and impose themselves as speakers and actors on the affirmed progression of events. Within the autobiographical framework of the book they are the means of establishing a plurality of agency, and a substructure of anecdotal verification, that seem harder and harder to come by in our subsequent fiction—neither the testamentary deposition nor the various free-standing mechanisms of comic-strip or science-fiction fabulation appear capable of these decisive effects—and that can begin to trouble us by their never quite dissembled absence from the argumentative design of Wallace Stevens's poetry.

This openness to the reality of other lives is fundamental to *Cancer*'s claim to be taken seriously as a tract for the age; for, all countergestures aside, Miller clearly writes as a birthright participant in that main American lineage of ministering fabulists described briefly in chapter two. In due course his readers would come to visit him as they visited Whitman, not to express literary-critical respect but to be told how to live. What he sees as a terminal crisis in the total system of world society is also, closer to hand, a crisis in active selfhood, in the individual human creature's purchase on life itself. "'I see myself dying again,'" his old friend Boris announces, suddenly turning up after months of unexplained absence; "'I *am* dying.'" Which, for Boris at least, has the comfort of a fact you can hold on to: "'Things happen so fast nowadays'" (151). And it is a first fact about human behavior, Miller implies, that we do take hold, on whatever terms are offered us. The "world" that has been dying all around us for a hundred years and more is, after all, "*our* world" (24), a habitat for actual people who either do or do not go on eating, talking, listening and observing, seeing friends, sleeping, screwing, looking for jobs—and writing, and reading, books. To Miller as to the Concord Transcendentalists a century earlier, there is one thing worse than death, and that is inaction, paralysis, nonbeing. "More obscene than anything is inertia" (225). It may well be that "we're all dead, or dying, or about to die," but what of that? We still need acts of imagination—and full stomachs ("good titles," "slices and slices of meat" [36]). We need most of all to keep a grip on present fact, and not lose sight of serviceable behavioral distinctions nor neglect reserves of real energy.

Thus it may only be "as far as history goes" that we experience ourselves as dead (90). Or only in the paralytic aggressions of our spiritual life. Miller gives the whole question the full antinomian, anti-idealizing twist. This everywhere visible fact of death is the death only of historical man, spiritual man, and Miller is happy about it because it may at last clear the way for the coming to life of the physical and sensual being in man. To acknowledge this fact in all its enormity may be the decisive step toward the true visceral-genital democracy of future times—in case anyone survives to enjoy it—or at least toward the only moral freedom that corresponds to physical actualities. (I am not here endorsing Miller's vision, only describing it.) If men and women are to find any happiness at all, it will be in the wholly natural pleasures of life, including the pleasure of naming openly the deepest of our fears.

That is, if we are truly to fulfill ourselves, it must be in ways that we can count on. First, in eating, filling our stomachs. The one impulse or motive Miller never trifles with is hunger; and this is how he differs from someone like Boris, who "never attached much importance to the food problem" but tries instead to nourish himself, and everybody else too, "with ideas" (153). To Miller a solid meal is worth anything: panhandling (or pandering; he does both), cutting moral corners with friends, even taking a succession of miserable jobs. And of course there is sex; but here matters are less simple. For the catastrophes that issue from contemporary degradation and dehumanization have overtaken sexuality as well, and they extend from syphilis and the clap (universal metaphors in the book, along with cancer and bed-lice, for the sickness of the historical world) to the mechanized rituals of "cunt-chasing" and the next lay that Miller's friend Van Norden is grotesquely caught in. As opposed to an artsy intellectual like the playwright Sylvester, whose life passes in a micturant dribble of talk, Van Norden is a figure of disturbing pathos. He is the character Norman Mailer seems to have had most in mind in describing Miller as the terrifying poet of modern sexual lust, the whole human organism breaking down into mechanized functions, or malfunctions.[6] The latter metaphor—Van Norden, on a sexual rampage, as "a machine whose cogs have slipped" (129)—is of course Miller's own and basic to the book as a whole.

The metaphoric argument of *Tropic of Cancer* ranges, in its articulation, from the ambiguous to the self-contradicting. But the book's imaginative poetry comes, surely, from its getting such contradictions into the open. What is still impressive is Miller's real freedom to give himself away, to bring into full view the argument with himself his narrative rises from. As is usual with an American writer, the affair has its self-consciously American aspect. In my incurable animal health, Miller declares, one foot in the rot and poison of historical Europe and the other in my own weird optimism, "I'm a bit retarded, like most Americans" (45).* To be American is to suffer from "arrested development" (138). Or it is to hold charter membership in a pack of senile children who are thoroughly inured to "violence and confusion" and therefore quite capable, as self-interest may direct, of "pulling the whole world down about our ears" (277). We notice in any case that the one fixed office in the antiroutine of Miller's life in Paris—one even more absolute than scheming for the next meal—is the daily trip to American Express for news or funds or whatever. It is the silver cord he never considers cutting.

But some such primordial linkage, he would say (none too precisely) is universal, a chain forged and reforged in the common misery of life:

Each one bound to the other. A fear of living separate, of staying born. The door of the womb always on the latch. Dread and longing. Deep in the blood the pull of paradise. The beyond. Always the beyond. It must have all started with the navel. They cut the umbilical cord, give you a slap on the ass, and presto! you're out in the world, adrift, a ship without a rudder. You look at the stars and then you look at your navel. You grow eyes everywhere—in the armpits, between the lips, in the roots of your hair, on the soles of your feet. What is distant becomes near, what

---

*Isn't this because he comes from a country, and knows it, which has never yet become fully nurturing to the selves who live in it? "It doesn't exist, America. It's a name you give to an abstract idea" (187).

is near becomes distant. Inner-outer, a constant flux, a shedding of skins, a turning inside out. You drift around like that for years and years, until you find yourself in the dead center, and there you slowly rot, slowly crumble to pieces, get dispersed again. Only your name remains. (258–259)

Yet the worst of it all is not cosmic aimlessness and obliteration, whose drastic breaching of every humane illusion clearly satisfies Miller. Rather it is consciousness, especially self-consciousness. As a character in the narrative, Miller has freed himself of this burden more than most. His friend Carl, as blocked with a new woman as he is with a transparently unwritable book, is envious and somewhat in awe of him. "'You only think about food,'" Carl accuses; "'*I think of everything*'" (106).[7] Such indeed is true damnation in Miller's antinomian vision—to be unable to close off reflexive consciousness—and feverish Van Norden is its principal victim. "'I wish to Christ,'" says Van Norden, "'that I could stop thinking about myself'" (97). And:

"Come around anyway, because I go nuts talking to these foolish cunts. I want to talk to you about Havelock Ellis. Jesus, I've had the book out for three weeks now and I haven't looked at it.... Would you believe it, I've never been to the Louvre—nor the Comédie-Française. Is it worth going to those joints? Still, it sort of takes your mind off things, I suppose." (96–97)

There is a hell for Miller, and this is it: the hell of being unable to take your mind off anything. This is why heroism has vanished from the contemporary world: "We know too much, maybe" (129). More generally, it is the hell of selfhood, which is both prison and life sentence. For almost everybody except, intermittently, Miller himself, there is no greater fear than that of being locked up inside one's own mind. What drives Van Norden to assault every woman within reach is the impossible hope that there must be one somewhere who can take him out of himself, and he despises them all because this is the one thing they cannot in fact do for him; they can only give him their imperfect selves. They've "'got to be better than I am,'" he angrily insists (118), and of course within his single definition of *better* they are not.

Against this double mechanization of world history and self-referential consciousness, various ways are indicated of immunizing oneself. One is to beat modern life at its own game by hiring on as an adjunct machine at the very center of its relentless signal-flow. This is the beauty to Miller of his job as proofreader on the Paris *Herald,* scanning for typesetters' errors without the least expense of reflective thought and in the process transmitting to others the catastrophes of contemporary life in even purer form than they had when they occurred (132–137). "I am a writing machine," he has said earlier of his own unprocessed transcriptions of reality (25); but marking proof sheets, shuffling "commas, semi-colons, hyphens, asterisks, brackets, parentheses, periods, exclamation marks, etc.," represents a strategic advance. The wholly mechanical refraction of this daily exposure to the world's lethal terrors effectively inoculates him against them.*

A surer way—since for the sake of ever stricter economies the management can, and soon does, simply abolish his cosy "blind alley" of a job (136)—would be to drop out altogether from the lockstep of everyday life, the licecrawl of "moralities and codes . . . platitudes and isms" (231). And drop into—what? Here, at some cost to expository coherence, the book's argument turns aggressively mythic. Miller is not himself an Aquarian; a Gemini rather, as seems appropriate for someone attempting, however absurdly, to be his own shadowy Other and to assimilate into his habit of life any new phenomenon that appears to menace it. But the base metaphor, in *Tropic of Cancer,* for escape and for recovery as a living being is alternately that of plunging into the waters of an impersonal reality, into "oceans that destroy and preserve at the same time," into the unceasing current of "everything that flows" ("rivers, sewers, lava, semen, blood, bile, words, sentences" [232–233]), or else of deliberately flooding the self with the same universal streaming: "the whole damned current of life flowing through you" (40).

Neither action guarantees future safety; sooner or later everyone drowns or strangles. The flow itself could not care less. But at least you are *in* life while

---

*In combination with the rest of *Tropic of Cancer* Miller's account of this job would appear to offer, before the fact, a refinement of Camus's formulaic description of the essential occupations of modern man: fornicating and *proof*reading the newspapers.

you live, and it is in you. And this to Miller is the ecstasy of sex, providing you are not obliged, like Van Norden, to sacrifice even this to the ravenings of ego-consciousness. The virtue of a good-hearted whore like Germaine, as Miller sentimentally sings her praises (39–43), is oddly like the virtue of the "good proofreader" (133). She, too, "is in the [ordinary] world but not of it," and appears God-like, no less, in her detachment, her impersonal devotion to getting the job done right. That "whole damned current" flows through you because it is also flowing selflessly "through her, through all the guys behind you and after you"—"all the men she's been with and now you, just you"—and so through "the flowers and the birds and the sun streaming in and the fragrance of it choking you, annihilating you" (40).

In communion with this truly anonymous and universal force of being—wherein is neither personal honor nor pride, conscience nor worldly ambition—"all mean egotism vanishes," or so Miller might well have written if Emerson had not written it first. The Emersonian set of *Tropic of Cancer* is not confined to its epigraph and choice of form. Late in the book we do in fact get a passage effectively reproducing the sustained episode in Emerson's *Nature* (chapter I) where that transcendent moral assertion is made: the famous episode of a solitary walk across a bare common, without any special good fortune of circumstance or thought, which Emerson offers in proof of all the reasonings to follow and in which, too, the same submission to universal currents of being furnishes the ecstatic climax ("I am nothing; I see all"). For Miller, however, in the night streets of Dijon, what secures the moment is not simply the totalization of his own miraculous sense of well-being but the presence of two other people who share the place with him, two lovers who stop, embrace, and walk along again: "I could feel the sag and slump of their bodies when they leaned against a rail, heard their shoes creak as the muscles tightened for the embrace" (256–257).

That is an image of relational life worth remembering when we turn back to the visionary climax of *Tropic of Cancer*, in the section just preceding: a long, erratically Nietzschean passage about the world's being reduced to zero in the obscene mechanization of even the generative mysteries, and about the countervailing desire, or will, to plunge directly into the incestuous and suicidal flow toward death and dissolution (216–233). The book's rhapsodic acceptance in such passages of a counterethic of "inhumanity," and its incidental equation of criminality and general "holocaust" with ecstasy and sainthood, cannot be glossed over as mere satiric extravagance or conversational high spirits. Neither should its casual rant about living happily as a beast of prey and—now that history has betrayed everybody—taking up bayoneting, rape, and cannibalism as regular pastimes (89–90). As with other major instances in the American tradition of antinomian counter-aggression, the moral affirmations and tolerances in *Tropic of Cancer* deserve the critical attention they cry out for (as well as against).

The problem here of imaginative consent is not

simply the one Orwell put his finger on, that under twentieth-century conditions "to say 'I accept' . . . is to say that you accept concentration camps, rubber truncheons, Hitler, Stalin" and so forth; accept them, condone them, identify your own survival with the historical "solutions" they represent (and in 1940 Orwell had not yet learned the half of it).[8] It is rather that on the plain narrational level of people's ordinary treatment of each other, *Tropic of Cancer* gives the appearance of endorsing this self-serving inhumanity as a legitimate rule of life. The narrator himself falls in with it when it serves his turn, or when he wants a quick and easy way of helping out importuning friends.

The spotting of *rape* in the middle of that short list of licensed counterterrors is one detail in particular that three or four decades of intersexual consciousness-raising have made a bit harder to let pass, at least publicly. Let it be said, though, that Miller's treatment of the war between the sexes is not the matter chiefly at issue. The question of how *Tropic of Cancer*'s language about women might look and sound to women readers certainly needed raising; but once raised, it yields, I think, to an ordinary awareness of how mimetic satire conventionally exorcizes the pathologies recorded. As a question about the mind of the book's producer it is fairly easily answered. Miller clearly reveres the beauty and power of female sexuality, and of ordinary womanly sweetness and practicality as well, and decries the violation of these qualities in the circumstance of modern life. It is much more commonly the male characters in his narrative vaudeville who are ridiculed and despised. If sex wars continue, women would not go far wrong in relying on the book's understanding of the combined intransigence and vulnerability of the ordinary male enemy. There is in fact a moment in the text when the character "Henry Miller" frames the perfect counterquestion to the sexist query and putdown made famous by Freud himself. Hearing out Van Norden's tirade about what it is that a woman "wants"—"they want your soul too"—Miller replies, "But what is it you want of a woman, then?" (117–118).

In any event I notice that in the shrewdest of New Feminist statements by American writers, Mary Ellmann's *Thinking About Women* (1968), it is not the synecdoche of woman-as-cunt that is morally challenged but the episode in which Miller robs a whore (whose odd temperament has given him fits) of not only her proper fee for the evening but of all the other money he digs out of her purse. Robs her and seems to claim credit for having done so. Breaking agreements and promises, helping friends dodge personal obligations, taking French leave whenever the equilibrium of his own life is threatened: these are the apparently self-legitimating acts which fill out most of the book's narrative sequences. Appropriately, *Tropic of Cancer* closes with a second episode of thievery and personal betrayal, in which Miller persuades his ugly-American friend Fillmore (whose fine "sense of adventure" depends on having the funds to buy his way out in case of trouble) that it will be easy to cut and run from his French fiancée;

then pockets for his own use the twenty-eight hundred francs of conscience money Fillmore, America bound, has made him promise to send the girl by telegraph.* Back safely in his own corner of Paris, Miller does think "for a moment" of poor Ginette. Conveniently, though, she comes to mind "sobbing and bleating, in that beastlike way of hers." So much for her. Then "a great peace" comes over him, and he drifts once more into thoughts of flowing rivers and high mountains, the particular amount of space or distance all human beings need in order to appear neither "negligible" nor "ugly and malicious" to one another, and how (it is the book's final sentence) the "course" of the river's flowing is, after all, "fixed" (278–287). Has the egotistical sublime ever rounded out its self-serving fiction with a balder, more absolute complacency?

3

If just here we were to put in evidence various late poems of Wallace Stevens—"The River of Rivers in Connecticut," perhaps, where, exactly as in *Tropic of Cancer,* the "fateful" river is "space-filled" and reflects all the seasons and also "the folk-lore / Of each of the senses," and in its mere flowing is a flashing "gayety," "a curriculum," and "a vigor"—we

*In 1930, roughly one hundred twenty dollars, a sum one could survive on for several weeks, with luck. This is hardly the first instance in standard fiction of cut-and-run narrative solutions or of the narrative *topos* of personal betrayal. Both are staples of Hemingway's storytelling, to name only one conspicuous precedent. But it may be the first in which neither remorse nor self-extenuation plays the least part in the total narrative economy.

would be touching on only one possible aspect of the literary-historical kinship between Miller and Stevens.*[9] Romantic titanism is only one of their changes of garments. For both writers the overbearing issue of individual survival in a world that may be aggressively indifferent to any such outcome is both a theme of themes and an unappeasable personal stimulus to fresh elaborations.

The result for each is an exceptional copiousness and yet repetitiveness of essential statement. So, too, without greatly shifting our focus, we might start with their convergence on a certain grandly inclusive conception of literary form. Near the beginning of *Tropic of Cancer* (20–25) Miller describes the new kind of book that he and Boris have been planning and that, with or without Boris, "has begun to grow inside me." It will be nothing less than a new Bible, and therefore must be written "anonymously"; that is, it will not express individual genius but will serve instead as the vessel into which everybody alive who has anything at all to say can pour it forth. Thus it will be, in effect, a book of what the personality-transcending imagination of humanity itself might have to say across the whole extent of the modern age and for a thousand years to come. It will be a "cathedral," no less, "in the building of which everybody will assist who has lost his identity"; everybody, in other words, who has already shaken

---

*Those poems of Stevens's cited here that are not in *The Collected Poems of Wallace Stevens* (New York: Alfred A. Knopf, 1954) may be found in *The Palm at the End of the Mind*, ed. Holly Stevens (New York: Alfred A. Knopf, 1971).

free of the straitjacketing of modern personalized self-regard. Its title will be—what else?—*The Last Book*.

Even earlier in *Tropic of Cancer,* with the sentence, "This is not a book" (1), Miller has set about establishing his claim to the mantle of Walt Whitman, the American poet who first thought to amass everything he might "promulge" into a single text coextensive with life itself and forming a new syllabus of collective regeneration. Stevens, in providing a first clue to his own poetic imperialism, kept his voice at a lower pitch and stayed closer to an established idiom of authorial self-description. It was not his way to advertise what he had written or meant to write as "a gob of spit in the face of Art," or as a bomb which would blow the whole contraption of existing culture to smithereens (*Cancer,* 2, 24). Yet the remarkable title—*The Grand Poem: Preliminary Minutiae*—he was urging on Alfred Knopf some months before the publication of *Harmonium* in 1923 is not modestly conceived. The second half of it only slightly diminishes its presumption. Correspondingly, in his old age Stevens, who resisted the idea of a collected edition until he had effectively stopped writing poems,[10] remained faithful enough to his original purpose to want to call the book *The Whole of Harmonium,* as if readers would remember what such a title retrospectively signified. This "Grand Poem" would do something more than express the individualized sense of the world that Stevens defined, in the lecture, "Effects of Analogy" (1948), as any poet's proper subject. Rather it would represent the poem poetry itself might create if released from all accessory obligations; if freed to become, as he had repeatedly proposed, its own true *subject* ("The Man with the Blue Guitar") and *supreme fiction* ("A High-Toned Old Christian Woman"). It would be that "essential" or "central" poem described in "A Primitive Like an Orb": that "huge, high harmony" which is both "the poem of the whole" and "the poem of the composition of the whole"; thus it would also stand as a "miraculous multiplex" of all lesser poems, and a "prodigious . . . patron of origins." Not even *The Cantos* or *Finnegans Wake,* in modern literature, proposes so absolute and final a life enterprise of collective fulfillment—or "fulfillment of fulfillments," to use yet another phrase from "A Primitive"'s litany of self-definition.

Or consider that Nietzschean "inhumanity" flaunted by Miller as proof of his transcendent seriousness: "I have nothing to do with the creaking machinery of humanity—I belong to the earth." By sheer force of desire he projects himself into that other race of superior beings, "the inhuman ones, the race of artists . . . always clutching and grasping for the beyond, for the god out of reach" (*Cancer*, 229–231). It is hard to find a phrase Miller deploys in this titan vein which is without its manifold counterpart in the Stevens of "Notes Toward a Supreme Fiction" and after. The expressive idiom is of course audibly different. But the essential imaginative correspondence seems to me as pronounced as it is with that earlier pairing of bluff vernacular declamation against an inexhaustible will to elaborate and refine represented in our literature by Mark Twain and Henry James: polar opposites, it once seemed, whom a half century of intensely partisan criticism has only bound closer and closer together in their characteristically American vision of disaster. Stevens's studied naturalism does not stop with *Tropic of Cancer*'s simplifying assertion of the superiority of physical reality to all those paralyzing "laws, codes, principles, ideals, ideas, totems, and taboos" (225) with which humanity has denatured itself in times past. But it is nevertheless Stevens among our poets whom we find declaiming in his final phase that "the great poems of heaven and hell have been written and the great poem of earth remains to be written," and who insists, in a poem of the same moment, "It is the earth itself that is humanity."[11]

I hope that what I have to say about Stevens's poetry in its relation to the diminished outlook of our own historical period will not be taken as some sort of accusatory brief or exercise in detraction. That he has emerged in recent years as academic criticism's indispensable modern poet is no more to be held against him than earlier election to that dubious role should have been held against Eliot or Yeats, though it pretty clearly was. Certainly I have no disagreement with Northrop Frye's tribute to Stevens, in an essay of 1957 that misses no part of his incantatory charm and courage, as "one of our small handful of essential poets" (nor for that matter with Professor Frye's backdoor readmission of *evaluation*, with the word "essential," and *historicity*, with the word "our," into the counsels of systematic criticism).[12] How essential Stevens could be to my own pleasure in poetry I found out when *Transport to Summer* was published in 1947 and I discovered soon after that I had much of it by heart. The lexical, pictorial, argumentative vividness of poem after poem (by a poet whom Delmore Schwartz described in 1955 as having "made the art of poetry visual in a way it has never been before"); the exhilarating balance of ceremoniousness and festival wit, of expansive sonority and precise aphoristic closure; the lifelong devotion to themes of a singular nobility and conceptual uniformity, and the poignancy of their final "edgings and inchings" in old age; the whole cumulative pathos of a poetry of mind whose dominating principle would turn out to be, "It can never be satisfied, the mind, never"[13]—these qualities have made the business of absorbing oneself in Stevens and taking inventory of the imposing mass of his work uniquely satisfying to a growing legion of commentators. And who will blame them? In as bad a time as we think ours has become—bad, it seems, for an "essential" poetry as well as for human anticipation in general—what better way is there for finely trained spirits to keep a decent measure of imaginative confidence and hope?

Happily this abundance of critical commentary makes unnecessary another descriptive outline of Stevens's poetic universe. If scores of essays on Stevens and at least a dozen well-argued books had accomplished nothing else, they would by now have served to make the great back-and-forth argument of his poetry—more exactly, the words and phrases chiefly positioning this argument in consciousness—a kind of lingua franca among his more faithful readers. Stevens's verse-making authority has proved to be of that self-validating kind which has power to set the terms of its own acceptance and which controls for a time the very language of critical discussion. Is there any doubt that something like this has taken place? Is there a serious book or essay about Stevens since c. 1960 which does not fall to talking Stevensese at its affirmative climaxes, securing key arguments by means of those same words and phrases?—"poverty" and "our climate," the "interior paramour" and the "plain sense of things," the "Snow Man," the "great poem of winter," the "scholar of one candle," the "cure of the ground," the "mythology of modern death," "repetition," "resemblance," "major man," "the first idea," or, in characteristic oppositional form, "what will suffice" versus the "fatal, dominant X"; the "total affluence" versus the "total leaflessness."

But the other side of such tributes by assimilation is that while they continue, they may effectively close off a writer's work from normal questioning of its distinctive "sense of the world," its whole imaginative scope and prepossession. With Stevens, questions as to what general conception of experience—including the experience of poetry—we commit ourselves to if we do accept him as an essential poet, need to be asked more insistently than I think has been the rule in recent discussions. (I assume this can be done without curtailment of pleasure in the poetry itself.) The "need to realize poetry," Stevens wrote in 1945 with that slight telegraphic oddness of his, is simply "the desire to contain the world within one's own perception of it."[14] But is that indeed what the poetic impulse essentially amounts to where we most value it, and, if so, what "perception" of the world does it issue from in Stevens's own case? And what force shall we grant the judgment from our own time's beleaguered effort to "realize" poetry?—it comes in Berryman's tribute to Stevens in *The Dream Songs*—that there is an "odd/ ... something ... something ... not there in his flourishing art"; that though he is beyond question "better than us," he is all the same "less wide."[15]

The idea of the "inhuman" as necessary to imaginative fulfillment offers one point of entry in this matter. Particularly after 1940 (though the idea is first roundly articulated in "Sunday Morning") a dialectic of "human" and "inhuman" enters with some regularity into Stevens's meditations and verse pageants, where it takes on the same kind of elusiveness and propositional ambiguity, poem by poem, as attaches to the broader dialectic of "imagination" and "reality." Something appears to be lost, the poems tell us, when we become "wholly human" and "know ourselves" only within those limits. The "inhuman" as such may not be the object of our ordinary seeking. It may rather be the special realm of the gods and demons of times unrecoverable, if not of mere effigies and abstractions; it may be something arrogant and intractable in the frame of life itself that will not rest until, "[making] choice of a human self," it "pierces ... with strange relation"; or it may be a destructive potentiality within the human imagination's own "forms of dark desire." Yet to be without the "inhuman" is to be fixed in a particularly ominous condition of "poverty." The death of Satan *was* "a tragedy/ For the imagination"; the unbreakable "rock" *is* man's "gray [or green] particular," both the "stone from which he rises [and] the step to the bleaker depths of his descents...."[16] The risks accepted in speaking in this fashion are not dodged. Indeed Stevens's intensifying preoccupation with such risks is a great part of what kept him turning each new poem, however brief, into a fresh counterposing of conceptual alternatives. How he would have liked the argument to resolve itself seems clear enough. The transfiguring giant of poetry (as described in particular in the beautiful "Chocorua to Its Neighbor" of 1943) is to be "fetched out of the human mountain"; his shadow will be "a human thing," and he will "speak humanly from the height or from the depth/ Of human things."

But even here we notice that the primary figure for this reiterated humanness is not of any actual company of diversified temporal beings but of the unitary mass of a "mountain," and we recall that other propositional equation that "it is the earth itself that is humanity." Stevens, of course, speaks so abundantly on what philosophically matters to him that he can be quoted or paraphrased against himself on almost any major issue; the more so because his fine instinct as a maker of poems is to turn every new statement into the autonomous "cry of its occasion."[17] And poetic occasions do differ. So I would agree with Frank Kermode that one much-cited entry in the prose *Adagia*—"Life is an affair of people and not of places. But for me life is an affair of places and that is the trouble"—cannot be taken as conclusive since it is too readily offset by others affirming the true poet's categorical "humanity."[18] Correspondingly, a remark in the last months of Stevens's life that he had long thought of adding a fourth section to "Notes Toward a Supreme Fiction," to be called "It Must Be Human," is not necessarily a confession of failure nor even a repudiation of the poem's opening proposition, "It Must Be Abstract."

The real question, however, is not about the attributive theory of value that can be assembled from Stevens's writings but about the relational world or society propounded within the poems themselves. Does this world exist in imagination as anything other than a mental space in which the human self observes the back-and-forth progressions of its interior history? Not that these progressions are wanting a rich affective interest of their own. The phenomenal sequences of Stevens's poetry swarm with exaltations and abysses, imperilments and recoveries, fillings and emptyings, the bliss of the familiar and the terror of the remote and alien;[19] and its projection of endlessly alternating mental states and gestures is worked into particular poems with a mesmerizing fertility of local invention.

Yet listening to it all in another way, we may begin to sense a poverty or emptiness of a different sort. It is, in a word, an unpeopled poetry. It is, of course, full of specified personages: not only exotic Bonnies and Josies, Nanzia Nunzios and Canon Aspirins, but a shadowy household of fathers, mothers, brothers, sons, spouses, true sympathizers, well-dressed men and ordinary women, ephebes, soldiers, skeletons, revolutionists, rabbis, assassins. But these are basically tableau-figures, surrogates for unchanging forms of desire and understanding. One by one, or even two by two, they do not alter the impression of, in Helen Vendler's words, a "narrowness," "a world excessively interior";[20] for they neither communicate directly with each other nor show us how they have separately come forward into their affirmed identity.

These figures enter the poems as symbols for imaginative positions already taken; they are not free agents who might contribute answers of their own to the parable-arguments they are devised to illustrate. That absence of "the reek of the human" which even Professor Kermode begins by acknowledging[21] is specifically, I would say, an absence of those extended temporal and passional relationships in which feeling not only discovers its inherent value-to-itself but enters a fully participatory second life in the exchanges of an actual life history; and in which speech, too—for the matter, as it remains to say, is also stylistic—passes beyond the repetitions and tautologies of self-predication into a dramatized necessity and impulsion.* Stevens's poetry is a

---

*Kermode's counterassertion on the point of Stevens's "humanity" is interestingly undercut by its own precision of phrasing: "No poet ever wrote so fixedly from within the human head as Stevens" (*Wallace Stevens* [Edinburgh: Oliver and Boyd, 1960], p. 20). Writing from within the human head, in the common sense of the phrase, is not the same as writing from within the relational dramas of collective or even personal existence. The poetry of encapsulated visionary intervals, and not of generated actions augmenting our passional consciousness of what is actually in store for us in life; for it seems axiomatic to me that passion enters, and human life undergoes those changes of state by which alone it knows itself, only as two or three, at least, are gathered together in experience and with whatever distressing inharmony speak, listen, and act in their own right, their own progressive determination.

Stevens's vigorous intelligence pushed the discovery of such encapsulated moments, and the symbolic hypotheses that spill down from them, to the last brink or precipice of the actantial—which is to say, to the point where a reawakened desire for shared action produces almost unrecognizable "images" of itself and "forms that speak."[22] Certainly he admitted into his poetry ideas of human action at its most convulsive and transforming: the idea, for one, of erotic aggrandizement, and equally of the wars and rumors of war which coincided with his two periods of greatest productivity (1914 to 1922, 1935 to 1950). But considered in themselves as fields of imaginative action, the poems lack, so to speak, a circumstantial society of their own adequate to the ideas that or-

---

extraordinary power of a Wordsworth, master of the Anglo-American egotistical sublime in secular form, is in attaching this argument about "the imagination's life" to concretely rehearsed episodes in an actual lived development (for what is the sublime itself, in modern literature, but an attempt to fill a void of objectless anxiety created by societal disruption and deprivation?). Philosophically—and poetically—considered, Wordsworth is both more circumstantial and more candid than Stevens.

ganize them (so William James criticized the arguments of Santayana, Stevens's philosophic master.) The only truly generative relationship is between the self's apprehension of its intrinsic power and its apprehension of some vast realm of being which is indifferent to that power if not actively arrayed against it.[23]

And it is sometimes precisely where the poems rise to a sustained affirmative climax that one finds oneself most conscious of what this absence and resulting emptiness can cost Stevens in full persuasiveness. To my mind, for instance, it simply is not true—though in 1947 I could take it for gospel, and still love to hear the words roll out—that "the greatest poverty is not to live / In a physical world": the opening of the eloquent final section of "Esthétique du Mal." Not true, that is, in the naturalistic senses of the word *physical* that come out of the poem itself, where the power and promise of the sun and the warmth of household familiars (sections vi and v, respectively) are understood as belonging to one and the same order of being. What seems more profoundly impoverishing, to consciousness and imagination, is not to live in a world of fully potentiated human exchange; a world in which the sharing of work and nurture and of a civil rather than simply cognitive or metaphysical ground of feeling and understanding is continuously active in common experience.

I hope it is understood that the matter centrally in question is not Stevens's choice of subject, nor is it his preference for an "elegiac" (his word) as opposed to dramatic treatment. The sense of narrowness seems to me stylistic as well, as it would have to be; if such an impression comes to us at all, it must come as a fact of language. The paradox with Stevens is that the argumentative amplitude and assurance of, especially, his later writing are at the cost of a palpable reduction in the practical resources of verse statement. There is no question that, particularly after 1940, his self-communing grew richer and suppler; and the poems it released beggar, in the comparison, nearly everything written since his death in the soliloquizing, observational-reflective (or confessional) mode. But the poetry in them does not so much speak its language as handle it, arranging and disposing it in hypnotizing relays of denomination and allusion. It is a poetry that, in particular, contracts the resources of the English verb into essentially copular and intransitive or reflexive forms—predications of identity, resemblance, location, cognitive apprehension, self-division and self-transformation—and that finds in sequences of appositional noun phrases a fully satisfactory way of organizing each verse sentence. The "something missing" Berryman speaks of is as much as anything else an openness to the whole kinesthetic power of language to convey the material process of human action and change; an openness first of all to the energy of a fully transitive syntax. In that last section of "Esthétique du Mal," for example, the proper verbs are *is* and *was*, *live*, *feel*, *tell* (in the sense of *distinguish*), *observe*, *experience*, *conceive*, *gleam*, *lie*, *think*, *see*, *find*, *propound*, *hear*, *make*, *occur*—verbs almost exclusively of being, cognition, sensory connection. No active exchange takes place, no impression of movement or reciprocation develops except within the observing intelligence itself. The passage as a whole remains at a reflective and summarizing distance from even these inward events and linkages (which is not to say that outlining the stages of interior reflection may not in itself be remarkably moving, here as elsewhere in Stevens).*

*Not a great deal has been written about this aspect of Stevens's writing and its poetic consequence (though Merle E. Brown has some good pages on the related matter of verse rhythm in *Wallace Stevens: The Poem as Act* [Detroit: Wayne State University Press, 1970], pp. 127–132). But not to hear this continual expressive distancing and immobilizing of primary experience, particularly in the later poetry, is to turn Stevens into another kind of poet altogether. Of a comparable climax, in "Notes Toward a Supreme Fiction," II, iv —

> The captain and his men
> Are one and the sailor and the sea are one.
> Follow after, O my companion, my fellow, my self,
> Sister and solace, brother and delight

—Harold Bloom has commented that it "ends by sounding like Hart Crane" (*Wallace Stevens*, p. 171). What a curious remark. Stevens will sound like Hart Crane, I think, only if you are reading by a process of conceptual paraphrase, substituting formulas of your own for his actual language. A passage in Crane which this comment would seem to bear upon is the second section of "Voyages," with a supplicative "O" in both its third and fifth stanzas. If we listen, though, to the actual voicing of Crane's lines—

> And onward, as bells off San Salvador
> Salute the crocus lustres of the stars,
> In these poinsettia meadows of her tides, —
> Adagios of islands, O my Prodigal,
> Complete the dark confessions her veins spell

—we hear among other activating elements two strongly transitive verbs, *salute* and *spell*, which hardly find a place in the whole

Especially in a critical era regressively preoccupied with ad hominem theories of literary history, there are temptations to say that this diminishment in syntactical force was Stevens's particular legacy—crippling and yet, in a constricted time, indispensably enabling—to the generation of American poets that grew up into the work of his last phase. For Stevens himself it seems to have been the means of establishing a controlled space to operate in, and a mediating idiom within which there was less risk of miscalculations of tone; less risk, too, of self-exposure and self-injury. That he wanted immensely to be somehow at the center of visible, discussible life and yet never have to give himself away to it—as Hart Crane, Yeats, Eliot, all finally risk doing—his letters and early journals (in the excellent editions Holly Stevens has assembled) make abundantly clear. Stevens was an extraordinarily private and guarded man, and there is a decided oddness about the life he himself seems to have settled for. In his mid-sixties he wrote in a family letter of his own father:

> . . . he was incapable of lifting a hand to attract any of us, so that, while we loved him as it was natural to do, we also were afraid of him, at least to the extent of holding

---

body of Stevens's work, and a third verb, *complete,* which is still fully transitive though more generalized in referential value and which Stevens never uses at all, except adjectivally. (These details may be verified in the appropriate entries in Thomas F. Walsh, *Concordance to the Poetry of Wallace Stevens* [University Park, Pennsylvania: Pennsylvania State University Press, 1963].)

off. The result was that he lived alone. The greater part of his life was spent at his office; he wanted quiet and, in that quiet, to create a life of his own.[24]

If we detect self-portraiture in this, Holly Stevens's editorial comment bears us out: "It certainly was true," she writes, "of my father and of our house as I grew up; we held off from each other—one might say that my father lived alone."[25]

The biographical details are fragmentary, yet fairly consistent in the impression they produce. A deep shyness or, better, self-guardedness is common enough in well-brought-up young men, whatever their choice of occupation. For one entering adult life in the middle-class America of the McKinley–Theodore Roosevelt era and determined on becoming a great poet or artist, it is positively predictable. But with Stevens habits of watchfulness and separateness seem carried to an extreme. Those solitary all-day walks in Stevens's early New York days—forty-two miles, he precisely records after one such, from four in the morning until half past six at night[26]—have the character of a disciplinary regimen, a testing of how much he could really take in of the visible world but also of moral stamina and self-sufficiency. Having three friends for company on one of these walks reduced its value to him: "I detest 'company' and do not fear any protest of selfishness for saying so."[27] The world at a distance was what he preferred, as from the brink of the Palisades looking down at roof tops and river activities far below him. People close up were "painful," "confusing beyond measure"; they "look at one so intimately, so stupidly." "I loathed every man I met, and wanted to get away...."[28]

In part, of course, in these journal passages, he is trying his hand as a writer, and allowance should be made for a normal degree of attitudinizing; but the same attitudes are displayed more objectively, too, as when at twenty, after the death of a young woman at whose home in the Reading countryside he had boarded, off and on, through the previous summer, he found the proprieties of condolence too difficult to manage: "I don't know just how I felt about it.... I did not dare to visit or to write her sisters."[29] And perhaps as important as any other set of private facts in the case of Wallace Stevens are those odd intimations of the character of his marriage and of the household circumstance of his life through the whole forty years of his maturity as a poet. Elsie Kachel Stevens was a woman of remarkable beauty but also of what seems an equally remarkable defensive severity. "All her life," Holly Stevens writes, "she suffered from a persecution complex which undoubtedly originated during her childhood, and which I was unable to understand for a long time."*[30]

---

*What was apparently as hard as anything to understand was Elsie Stevens's eventual distaste for the poetry itself. "While I was growing up," Holly Stevens continues, "my mother did not read my father's poems, and seemed to dislike the fact that his books were published" (Holly Stevens, *Souvenirs and Prophecies: The Young Wallace Stevens* [New York: Alfred A. Knopf, 1977], p. 226). It wasn't only Stevens's business associates from whom his activity as a poet remained sealed off, especially after he re-

It is hard to avoid concluding that Stevens himself shared in this wariness of personal exposure. Why *did* he, immediately following the success of his first book with readers who ought to have mattered to him (Marianne Moore for one, in her *Dial* review), all but abandon poetry for the next six years—ten years, really, there being the barest handful of new poems from 1930 to 1933—though interest in his work remained strong enough to warrant a second printing of *Harmonium* in 1931?[31] Did the birth of a child in 1924, and the onset of fatherhood, drain away his willingness to stand any deeper in hostage to actual life and fortune? He was working hard at his business occupations but not harder, so far as anyone has determined, than when the *Harmonium* poems were being written between 1913 and 1923. And there is no evidence that his business affairs were not prospering, securing his material position and future. Why then was it that the Stevenses chose, in effect, to camp out in a rather disagreeable neighborhood in West Hartford rather than settle themselves somewhere more satisfactory and permanent? For it is a fact that that great metaphysical declaration on the sources of poetry itself, "that we live in a place / That is not our own,"[32] a declaration

---

sumed it in the 1930s. Yet who can ever be sure that such everyday circumstances are matters of accident or fortune and not of instinctive personal choice? Did marriage for Stevens (as for his younger contemporaries Eliot and Faulkner) establish as a household familiar an intimately contrary muse whose presence was at once impassioning and obliterating?—to adapt two words used with special emphasis in the fourth stanza of "Sunday Morning."

widely admired as a statement of canonical truth, comes to us from a man who on an insurance executive's income lived with his wife and child as renters in a two-family house, enduring at his doorstep (as Holly Stevens remembers) the racket of a main out-of-town highway and the irritations of his landlord's noisy brood of children. Not until well past fifty did Stevens buy a house of his own. Coincidentally he began to travel less and less away from his home and his office, eventually giving up even the winter holidays in Florida that supplied imaginative themes for so much of his earlier poetry, as if increasingly fearing to interrupt the stabilizing routine of his daily existence. After Holly's infancy he and his wife seem to have preferred doing without domestic help and having no one else about the house. "The Stevenses shrink from everything," he wrote Barbara Church in 1948, staying on in Hartford through yet another humid Connecticut Valley summer.[33]

These biographical details, whatever one makes of them, in no way reduce admiration for the poetry itself and the sustained feat of invention it represents. If poetry is, as Stevens thought, not a "rather meaningless transmutation of reality" but "a combat with it,"[34] his artistic courage and resourcefulness will not appear the less because his actual conception of that "reality" proves queerer and more constricted than we might at first have thought—and more content with its own partialness. That Stevens's poetic achievement rises from a limited and self-limiting base in the exchanges of human experience and, moreover, leaves essentially unchallenged its own architectonic exclusions, does, however, make a difference to judgment. And by the measure of our regulative interest in the world of active human coexistence I find little to choose, finally, between Stevens and Henry Miller as visionary imaginations. Stevens, beyond question, is the finer, steadier artist, the one who more consistently translates his imaginative perception into some sharply pleasurable and, on its own terms, unimprovable figure of statement. But he is also the one who was satisfied to find his art's highest justification in its furnishing "sanctions" and "reasons for being" to the poet himself; in its securing him the "ecstatic freedom of mind which is his special privilege," and thus in providing, "in the last analysis," a better means of "*self*-preservation" (my emphasis).

This consummate rationale for the autonomy of the poet's vocation comes in the closing paragraphs of the lecture-essay, "The Noble Rider and the Sound of Words," which Stevens read at Princeton in May 1942, the same month in which he was completing "Notes Toward a Supreme Fiction." It says nothing that Henry Miller could not have subscribed to had he been listening, though it says it in a rather more stately and featureless idiom. Neither, in particular, would Miller have disagreed with Stevens's further suggestion that in a violent universe we may think of the artist's predicating imagination as an answering "violence from within." But Miller would not himself have completed this final formulation as Stevens did in fact choose to complete it: "a violence from within that *protects* us from a violence without" (my emphasis). In the abstract, or as a term in an invented argument, the desire for self-preservation and self-protection needs no special apology. Neither, I think, does Miller's equally abstract desire to dissolve into the current of "everything that flows" and be taken altogether out of the boundaried circumstance of a necessarily contingent selfhood. In each case what is literally proposed is a morality of subjective longing that answers to nothing beyond its own powerful imperatives, being relatively unmoved by any wider occasion of feeling, and that openly glories in the imagination's autochthonous power to create even "from nothingness" a mythological universe which primarily registers, as Stevens proclaims, the magnitude and attractiveness of that inward longing: "the heavens, the hells, the worlds, the *longed-for* lands."[35]

Both writers, it seems to me, went further than any of their extravagant American generation, further even than natural anarchists like Jeffers and Cummings, in relinquishing the hope of a self-fulfillment which would be collectively regenerative as well—and in finding it possible to get along quite happily without the consolation, or the protection, of that hope.[36] But it is Stevens in particular who, affirming personal survival as poetry's extraordinary prize, set the terms on which the next generation of American poets would address itself (but without the counterweight of his immense self-possession) to its difficult calling. No wonder he has come critically into his own in the confidence-shattered era that has succeeded him—though whether it is to be as (Harold Bloom's view) our century's greatest poet and singular glory or (Hugh Kenner's) the very oddest sort of proof of the final wearing out of Romantic egoism[37] is a question that still naggingly lacks a clear answer.

5
Prospects

> There is nothing to prevent our taking for granted all sorts of happy symptoms and splendid promises—so long, of course, I mean, as we keep before us the general truth that the future of fiction is intimately bound up with the future of the society that produces and consumes it.
>
> Henry James, "The Future of the Novel" (1899)

> The slightest return of beauty makes you aware how deep your social wounds are, how painful it is to think continually of nothing but aggression and defense, superpowers, diplomacy, terrorism, war. Such preoccupations shrink art to nothing.
>
> Saul Bellow, *To Jerusalem and Back* (1976)

Six months into the First World War, as the revolutionary scale of the conflict became daily more apparent, the poet Rilke wrote to a young friend serving in the Imperial armies concerning an unexpected performance at Leipzig of his prose-poem on the "love and death" of Cornet Christoph Rilke, written in 1899 when he was twenty-four: "So . . . my voice of fifteen years ago speaks into the listening ear of people who have been living in terror for months." In this wartime revival of a work from "one distant night of my youth" Rilke found oddly confirmed a phenomenon as disturbing to him as any material fact of the immense struggle itself; and that was the unprecedented voicelessness of the present time in its own behalf, under the widening shock:

> ... you notice again and again how dumb we have grown here. I am sure everyone is so at heart; even if a few must hear themselves and pluck their strings with this thought and that, there is no one who can draw sounds from the air that sweeps through him, not even to lament,—it is a silence of halted, interrupted hearts. I am certain no one loves in these days; however much one or another heart may achieve, it acts out of some sort of universal store of human kindness, warmth, willingness and resignation, it does not give what is its own, but behind every act primeval store-rooms of human need are expended; even you out there act and struggle out of strengths hoarded up in some such deposit of instinctive mutuality. It seems to me as though the heart in each of us were only passing things on, confined to gazing in astonishment at the store spilling through its hands.[1]

As the havoc of 1915 continued and spread, Rilke wrote again and again in this vein—and never simply about the latest news of destruction and suffering. The disturbing thing, he told another correspondent, "is not the fact of this war, but that it is being used and exploited" (i.e., by its too submissive human agents). It had become a sovereign daily business like any other, work which—once flung down upon the world—was now being carried on simply because it was there to be done; "people cling to it greedily, with all the weight of their heavy conscience."[2] In the crisis, certain perplexing portents and symptoms from the past returned to mind and were clarified. For the first time, Rilke told several friends, he could see how it was that "those two powerful old men, Tolstoi and Cézanne, went around and uttered warnings and threats, like prophets of an ancient covenant that is soon to be broken—and they did not want to live to see that break."*

It has not been my intention, in constructing this overview of our own extended moment in literature, to offer Henry Miller and Wallace Stevens as the prophetic Tolstoy and Cézanne of the latest stage of modern historical catastrophe; a stage which, though not centered as in 1915 in a single imagination-staggering world event, seems to us equally transforming, equally irreversible. But one might well propose Rilke's wartime letters as an essential prevision, from within the literary consciousness itself, of the fate of literary making in a radically self-revolutionized age. For what Rilke was essentially saying by late 1915 was that the fundamental circumstance of poetic responsiveness and recombination had itself broken apart. To any onlooking imagination the immediate world of present experience, plunging ever deeper into systematized self-violence, had become "almost impenetrable," yet appeared overwhelming in its own power to penetrate and coerce and to impose its terrible discipline: "Only

*To the Princess Marie von Thurn und Taxis-Hohenlohe, 2 August 1915. Writing to Helene von Nostitz, Rilke had specifically recalled Cézanne's outcry in the streets of Aix-en-Provence at some new report of life's immitigable violence: "Le monde, c'est terrible . . ." (Letter of 12 July 1915, *Wartime Letters of Rainier Maria Rilke*, trans. M. D. Herter Norton [New York: W. W. Norton, 1940], p. 35).

very rarely now, as if by mistake, does a thing speak to me, granting and giving without demanding that I reproduce it altogether equivalently and re-emphatically within myself"—this to Ellen Delp on October 27.

It was not that poetry itself had lost its immeasurable value. In this war atmosphere the poet's true mission appeared to Rilke as compelling as ever. To display the world of our existence not as if one were fixed numbly in bondage to it but with a portion of that freedom and conclusiveness of vision which in corresponsive fullness belonged to what he had learned to call, poetically, the "angelic" order—this, he felt, was surely his "real task." Yet the same dire atmosphere made the conditions for succeeding seem proportionately more remote and unattainable. "To begin that task, Ellen, how *protected* and *resolved* [my emphasis] one needs to be." But it was just such protectedness and inner resolution that the immense surge of the times was remorselessly destroying.

Perhaps we ask too much of our writers, clinging at some hidden level of expectation to the idea that what great literature finally can give us is somehow of a piece with what in our own lives (the oblique phrasing is Williams's, in "Asphodel") we may indeed be miserably dying for lack of. Be that as it may, Rilke's twentieth-century premonition of the virtual impossibility of this marvelous restorative gift is, we now recognize, no freak of crisis conditions. To us it will seem extraordinary only in its undiminished originality and clarity of statement. For the idea of some radical fracture of the kind

Rilke posited within that whole perceptual economy in which fresh creative utterance can be authentically nurtured; an economy necessarily privileged for those prepared to take advantage of it, but justified for them as they make use of it to recover something altogether indispensable, "the connection of the poet with his whole living generation"[3]—that idea reemerges now with every unflinching examination we make of present circumstances for life and work. The numbed siege mentality of 1915 has turned out to be not an unconscionable interruption of essential imaginative process but something much nearer its anesthetized norm.[4]

That some such perceptual economy and privilege are preconditions for major literary creation stands, I think, as an elementary truth of actual literary history. The arts appear categorically to require some accepted behavioral margin of tolerance and civil immunity, and some equally exempted foreground of preparation, in order to burgeon and flourish in any form. (Only a utopianism that, on the point of human regimentation, has everywhere betrayed its evasiveness, or worse, will continue to think otherwise.) And a civil culture capable of tolerating and balancing out its own structural contrariness—capable, that is, of genuine freedom—might well be defined as one that systematically, and consensually, licenses these open margins.* Our century, bad as its

---

*The plural here is intentional; at any given time there must be more than one such margin, according to the natural differentiae of age, sex, class, education, daily occupation, and the like.

tendencies may appear, has so far left open at least a bare strip of marginal space of this kind. Even in the circumstance of modern total war this enabling license has not been totally suspended. So Rilke's own poetic projects underwent further delays but continued their difficult incubation, and his extraordinary letters of 1915 and 1918 are, after all, a rare enough literary accomplishment: a free and conclusive statement, by a contemporary, of the lived character of a great human and historical disaster.

For the modern era in general—that is, since the full-scale consolidation of the contemporary urban-industrial order—a literary sociologist looking for the enduring sources of imaginative vitality and power might well conclude that what has persistently obtained in literary practice has been a kind of

---

Every theory of literature that is seriously addressed not only to art's cultural function after being produced (the humanist-educator's preoccupation) but equally to the conceptual and imaginative economy of its moment of production recognizes some such categorical requirement—from, say, Keats's idea of a disinterested "negative capability" which is essential to poetic greatness to Mikhail Bakhtin's argument, in *Rabelais and His World* (1965; trans. 1968), for modern art's antithetical origins in that festive perception of the world which rises from the carnival moment in the calendars of human activity, with its licensed reversals of the established hierarchy of life and value. For the preliterate masses these intervals of remission came, as Bakhtin reminds us, only at scheduled times. But for the leisured and crypto-clerical classes who since the Renaissance have been both the makers of our literature and its principal public, such remission from strict economic discipline, in the broad sense, becomes problematically chronic and normative, a burden of private freedom desperately needing to be reconstituted for humanly satisfying and productive use.

pastoralism of innovation and fulfillment, of fundamental health-in-work. I mean pastoralism here in its familiar topological sense. From its beginning as a calculated expressive strategy, pastoral fiction has always projected, at least implicitly, a double terrain of human activity and relationship. Here is the privileged retreat where the regulative conditions of life and work remain ideally proportioned to an individualized human resourcefulness. But over there, never out of sight, is the imperial capital itself, the very measure (and cause) of ethical, psychological, economic disorder and interruption. And in modern history it is demonstrably the case that our civilization's major capitals—the aggrandizing centers of political, economic, and intellectual authority—have been progressively less able to generate their own literary and imaginative succession. Rather they have imported renewal, insofar as renewal has occurred, from various exempted sectors or provinces; from imaginative environments, that is, where the peculiar exhaustions of our unprecedented era have not yet taken hold so massively and overwhelmingly.[5]

Within Anglo-American literature, the United States itself, from the time of Poe and Emerson to that of Eliot and Faulkner, may be seen as one of these exempted sectors. Not at all unimperial in political instinct or practice, the American consciousness could nevertheless conceive of itself, well into the present century, as essentially innocent of full imperial complicity; and though in the arts it remained persistently anxious about its exact degree of provinciality, it also displayed a rich confidence that in every vital respect (as Emerson told Carlyle in a famous exchange) it was playing the whole game "with immense advantage."[6] Like Eliot, and Pound, and (briefly) Frost, too, or like Henry James a generation earlier, an American writer might well conclude that he would have to leave the American province—as a place to do his work and have it intelligently received—in order to capitalize effectively on his birthright freedom of outlook. But not the least surprising part of the whole venture of expatriation would prove to be the relative ease with which he established performative authority once he had made his move—into cultural headquarters, so to speak, which no longer understood how to carry on their own self-appointed business.*

*Did, for example, any British literary figure in the nineteenth century after Byron and Scott have the same generative impact on European letters as the Americans Poe and Whitman? The answer is, yes, one: the adoptive cockney Dickens—an exception splendidly endorsing the general rule. Since 1890 Ireland, too, for literature in English, has served as this kind of privileged or pastoral enclave. It is a commonplace of historical description that modern English writing of major imaginative force has been almost exclusively the work of foreigners, exiles, and provincials. By and large our century is not likely to be remembered in literature for undertakings fostered originally in London and the principal universities—in contrast to the Elizabethan age, or to the successive eras of Milton, of Pope, of Fielding and Dr. Johnson, and even of Blake, Coleridge, and Keats. Certainly there is now a fair consensus that Yeats, Hardy, Shaw, Joyce, Lawrence, Eliot, Faulkner, Beckett weigh more and count for more, as writers and as historical influences, than Bridges, Housman, Forster, Woolf, Graves, Waugh, or even—though one may still hate to say so—Auden; all indispensable as writers and instructors, but all essentially clarifiers rather than reinventors of literary possibility.

The more we examine the historical economy of actual literary making, the more erratic its processes are likely to appear. When in the past has our major literature *not* emerged from specially favored pockets (if not whole James families) within the national experience; from unpredictable accidents of dislocation and reentry; from intemperate violations of cultural protocol, in ninety-nine cases abortive but in the hundredth inexplicably liberating? And when has this literature *not* come into being by way of a certain disregard of orthodox schooling, of regularized systems of preparation and preferment? When, that is, have our most valued writers not started from some disavowal, either elected or enforced, of approved procedures for vocation?—lapsed or guilt-driven patricians like Cooper, Melville, Edith Wharton; resentful orphans or half-orphans like Poe, Twain, Frost, Cather, Berryman; born outsiders like Dreiser, Jack London, Richard Wright (and every black author yet born, and nearly every notable woman); and above all, for sheer numbers, the discontented or noncompliant offspring of professional specialization: ministers' sons (Emerson, Stephen Crane, E. E. Cummings); officers' sons (Hawthorne, Henry Adams, Robert Lowell); doctors' and lawyers' sons (Hemingway, Dos Passos, Edmund Wilson) and daughters, too (Dickinson, Jewett, Welty, Rich); or the children of schoolmasters, academicians, public benefactors, who were themselves authors of a sort (the Jameses, Eliot, Ginsberg, Barthelme, Updike).

For each of the writers named, the individual pattern of emergence shows itself as irregular and unanticipatable. Nevertheless, the general process is clear enough, and conforms to familiar cultural rules of progression-by-antithesis. Given the persistence of any societal differentiation at all, may we not expect this process to continue, under adverse conditions as well as congenial, and the broad form of it to find new confirmation whenever and wherever the next literary resurgence takes place? But I suspect that will be an event in any case which those professionally committed to charting and classifying it, or to training fledgling talent to take part in it, will more obstruct than assist. For what seems most certain is that such resurgence cannot be pedagogically decreed and legislated, any more than it can be contracted for by trend-spotting editors. That is why its proving ground will not be the university, the house of refuge currently for so much of what passes for serious literature. Literary renewal, if it comes at all, is not likely to come from writing courses or poets-in-residence (and most surely not from self-promoting schools of academic criticism competing to fill the place of a vanishing poetic). If what indeed we are confronted with is a deepening societal sickness, the withdrawal of literature into universities is part of that sickness and cannot be its cure.*

*Here is Saul Bellow's comment, in 1971, after reading his way through a fresh set of literary quarterlies and little magazines:

> Most ... are university subsidized, as what is not these days. The university has become the sanctuary, at times the hospital, of literature, painting, music and theater [this is not in fact true as regards painting and dance, the two arts for which, in the United States, the era of 1945 to 1975 needs no general

The irony in this is self-evident, for the university in its perfected modern form was to serve not only as an alternative environment of thought within modern society's expanding network of practical demand but a countercommunity in which, within the several arts and sciences, each mind's capacity to find its own way forward might be generously, substantially encouraged. The university has largely become instead the place where those who have started out fastest and won the first round of accredited prizes go to prepare for absorption into that network on personally advantageous terms, in the process putting a screen of institutionalized privilege between themselves and the emptiness or void-freedom of contemporary life. (It is a commonplace that in a thoroughly corporatized society universities have grown less and less distinguishable as institutions from the main sources of their funding.)[7] And as the full macrosystem of institutional life tightens its grip and increasingly syncretizes its enormous power of assimilation, there seems to be less and less chance that isolated pockets of exception and divergence can survive except as themselves empty and null. There seems less chance, too, that the restorative anomaly of what is genuinely creative can still find free space to materialize and have its

---

apology]. It contains also computers, atom smashers, agricultural researchers, free psychotherapy, technocratic planners, revolutionary ideologists. It has everything, including Bohemia.... And what is art, in this bohemianized society? It is a toy. ("Culture Now: Some Animadversions, Some Laughs," *Modern Occasions,* Winter 1971, pp. 169–170)

growth. The virtual disappearance of independent publishers with access to more than localized distribution—publishers of the sort that sustained a Faulkner's extraordinary career—is indicative of the whole disheartening trend, and confirms the atrophy it symbolizes.

Where exception and divergence do occur and appear to have held their own, what specific encouragement are we given? Significantly, certain odd instances of a kind of workshop collaboration that in contrast to the university or business-office model is essentially unscheduled and preferment-free do stand behind some of the liveliest writing of the postwar era. Here I have in mind not only those eccentric communes of self-validation which have intermittently served the temperament of an Allen Ginsberg or Gary Snyder, or the personalized journalistic teamwork that has provided a training-ground for *New Yorker*-sponsored talents like John Updike, Donald Barthelme, Renata Adler, though these have been important and concretely productive. What also appears to have become an accepted adjunct to literary creation is some version of the "uniquely collaborative method of composition" (Stanley Kunitz's phrase for it) which supported the extraordinary productivity of Robert Lowell's last several years. Of Lowell, Kunitz writes:

He made his friends, willy-nilly, partners in his act, by showering them with early drafts of his poems, often so fragmentary and shapeless that it was no great trick to suggest improvements. Sometimes you saw a poem in half a dozen successive versions, each new version ampler and bolder than the last. You would recognize your own suggestions embedded in the text—a phrase here and there, a shift in the order of the lines—and you might wonder how many other hands had been involved in the process.[8]

Collaborations of this sort which nevertheless allow for an individualized performative resolution are common enough in other arts, as they are perhaps basic—to take a major post-1945 example—to the primacy of New York School painting. (They are of course fundamental to theater and dance.) Moreover they do not end with the initial creation of new works. Audiences, too, become a calculated part of the productive process. The whole impetus of contemporary American painting, according to its indispensable interpreter, Harold Rosenberg, has been toward collaboration of this further kind; the "psychic collaboration of the spectator" without which particular works cannot establish a definite identity, and the painter's own act of creation remains incomplete:

In terms of meaning [Rosenberg argued], this collaboration was the point of the painting: immersed in the possibilities of the artist's sign, the spectator could share the creative élan of bringing it to light. An Abstract Expressionist painting completed itself in making an artist of its spectator.[9]

And if among that flourishing poetic generation born in the United States between 1923 and 1928 it is Frank O'Hara whose poems more and more show signs of preserving the vitality and savor of their origins (as I think they do), his intense collaborative association with the principal New York painters of his time suggests itself as an essential cause. The ceremonies of participation and self-extension their manner of work systematically invited him to enter into helped him free his own voice from the peculiar interferences, as well as incitements, that an excellent university education had put in his way.

But O'Hara's verse, even at its best, was deliberately "minor"; and about the dense mass, in Lowell's case, of *Notebook, History,* and the autobiographical volumes that follow, the question of durability and autonomous power has yet to be faced. Stanley Kunitz's account is emphatic on the point that a concern about these poems' exact provenance eventually "did not seem to matter much, for the end product always presented itself as infallibly, unmistakably Lowellian."[10] That the poems are Lowell's own seems clear enough, but that their interest as poems will altogether survive the fading of Lowell's strong personal presence and legend is for the moment less clear. He, too, may be more secure in critical standing as a spokesman and representative than as a primary maker of literary history. Indeed with every name cited in the several preceding paragraphs, I think we have to acknowledge that what continues to hold attention is not this or that supremely accomplished masterwork, or series of masterworks, nor is it any single work which has become required reading within the public that critically matters. It is rather in each case a lengthening sequence of writings having the provisional value of a life record, a prolonged testament simply to the possibility of individual persistence and survival. The collaborative enclaves into which literary making has largely retreated seem themselves more and more absorbed into that enterprise of performative survival which led me earlier to speak of a practice of literature that is essentially by, and for, and mostly about, survivors, its participants hanging on as best they can against less and less favorable odds.

Or else, in those quarters where a literature of weight and moment has heretofore found its chief representatives, not really hanging on at all. A case can easily be made that the most impressive single books published during the last dozen years of American writing, those at least with the richest and solidest "field of action,"* are books which have come into existence altogether accidentally—like the edited oral autobiographies of Malcolm X (1965) and Nate Shaw (1974); or Mailer's *The Armies of the Night* (1968), that one among his chronicles of public happenings which he was not already under contract to write when he reached the scene; or (to complete a tetrad of prose narratives I would as expectantly return to as any from these years) Robert M. Pirsig's *Zen and the Art of Motorcycle Maintenance* (1974), a book that, according to the author's note it opens with, is as eccentric in origin as the other three. Each of these is, as a text, adjunctive to some independent combination of public and personal circumstance;

Field of action was Gide's term, in his working notebook for *Les Faux-monnayeurs*, for what is most important for the novelist initially to establish.

each is singular in its narrative formation and, so to speak, imaginatively inseparable from the events-in-the-world it records.

An adjunct literature then? A literature whose most interesting creations materialize by accident, each one the unforeseen by-product of some odd warp in the organizational aggrandizements of modern life? It would be the appropriate counterpart to that literature without qualities I have pictured our writers-by-vocation as withdrawing into. And for a time at least it may be, by default, the best we can hope for. More than ever the full prospect for literature seems consubstantial with the prospect for civil society in the large. At present this society in its American manifestation has grown to be uniquely powerful and influential in general human existence (though its consenting adult members seem more and more easily terrorized by visions of catastrophic dispossession). And one can understand well enough the immense temptation either to demonize such coordinated power and influence, seeing their coerciveness as irresistible, or else blank them out altogether as realities of everyday existence—and of ordinary relational consciousness. But what can either response lead to except an ever deeper surrender of freedom, and coincidentally an abdication of any hope at all for a serious or consequential literature?

Perhaps, though, there can be comfort for the long run in remembering that in Anglo-American literary tradition some such burden of civil concern has weighed more or less directly on our writers' fortunes since the traumatic fracture of the English Civil War and Puritan Revolution, and throughout the ideological conflicts that became their tenacious aftermath. (This is that aspect and consequence of our protestant, parliamentary, entrepreneurial civilization which with periodic reemphasis has regularly distinguished it—for all its leading share in the catastrophes of modern world history—from the main imaginative commitments serving European literary practice.) If such civil concern, in the richest sense, remains effectively in force, then what even more clearly is essential to our belief or disbelief in the future of a literature worth commemorating is our belief or disbelief in the survival of any sort of historical community where it could conceivably continue to be produced.

Any existing community, writes the philosopher-critic Peter Jones, can modify the conventions of expectation through which the literary texts that are produced within it have their cumulative meaning.[11] That in fact the extended literary community of our own historical era may already have done so—and done so, over the past thirty-odd years, in its own despite—is, I suppose, the moral this short book and its successive arguments have principally rehearsed.

Coda

A Note on the Influence of Tropic of Cancer

While *Tropic of Cancer* remained under legal ban (as it did in English-speaking countries from 1934 to 1961), reading it was a kind of civic duty. Like *Lady Chatterley's Lover* and, earlier, *Ulysses*, the book was accepted, with its camouflaged wrappers and Paris imprint, as a symbol of the continuing struggle for both artistic and spiritual liberation; to be for it was to declare oneself on the side of freedom in the arts and natural honesty in human self-awareness. In its odd combination of outrage and unconcern at the catastrophes of modern history, *Tropic of Cancer* also came to be seen as symptomatic of a deepening crisis in the outlook for civilization as a whole. Orwell's notable essay (cited above, chapter four) only confirmed its standing in this respect.

The book has, then, a clear and not dishonorable place in the fluctuations of expressed moral and cultural attitude in our century, and conceivably of political attitude as well. How important is it, in addition, for the history of literature? To list its most vocal early partisans—beginning with Anaïs Nin and Lawrence Durrell—may be to suggest that its specifically literary influence has been peripheral and secondary. Even where the metaphor of cultural "cancer" has been kept in service, as fairly continuously by Norman Mailer over the past twenty years, the book as a whole—written in the exclamatory first person—may not seem much more than broadly corroborative of ways of going about the business of being a writer which would have persisted in any case, deriving as they do from longstanding American tradition. Mailer himself, though remaining loyal to this icon of his own apprentice years and willing to affix the word *genius* to an anthology of Miller's writings, acknowledges that Miller's reputation in literary circles has been isolated and idiosyncratic. Criticism has left a "space" around him; his reputation survives but "in a vacuum." Even at the point of asserting that Henry Miller may have "influenced the style of half the good American poets and writers alive today," Mailer effectively reduces this influence to a matter of atmosphere and inspiration. He remarks:

It is fair to ask if books as different as *Naked Lunch, Portnoy's Complaint, Fear of Flying* and *Why Are We in Vietnam?* would have been as well received (or as free in style) without the irrigation Henry Miller gave to American prose. Even a writer as removed in purpose from Miller as Saul Bellow shows a debt in *Augie March*.

That is, Miller's writings, above all *Tropic of Cancer* ("far and away his best book"), encouraged others to take greater expressive risks, and worked generally to widen public tolerance and receptivity. But the title chosen as showing a "debt" turns out to be what is now commonly regarded as an important later author's least effective, most artificially constructed book.[1]

Writers absorbed (as both Mailer and Bellow have been) in registering the immediate moral and physical chaos of modern city life are writers of the sort we might expect to find at least abstractly sympathetic to Henry Miller. Expectably, too, for evidence of more substantial textual influence we can turn to Beat and neo-Bohemian writers of the 1950s and 1960s. Is *Tropic of Cancer* where Allen Ginsberg got the title for his breakaway poem?—"It may be that we are doomed, that there is no hope for us, *any of us,* but if that is so, then let us set up a last, agonizing, bloodcurdling howl, a screech of defiance, a war whoop! Away with lamentation!" (*Cancer,* 232). So, too, almost everything attributed to "Moloch," the devouring specter of Part II of "Howl"—"Robot apartments! . . . blind capitals! . . . granite cocks! monstrous bombs!"—has its place in *Cancer's* rich outpouring of prophecy and invective, though rather surprisingly the epithet itself does not turn up in Miller's text.

In general, the line seems clear enough that runs from Miller's evocations of nightwalking in Paris and, in other books, New York and his native Brooklyn ("heart of American emptiness")[2] to Ginsberg's "negro streets at dawn" ("Howl") or Bob Dylan's "ancient empty streets too dead for dreaming" ("Mr. Tambourine Man"). Between

Henry Miller, by the 1950s a fixture at Big Sur, and the California *jeunes sauvages* who went down the coast to claim him as patron, the correspondences, textual as well as biographical, are hard to miss. In part, perhaps, because Lawrence Ferlinghetti at City Lights too automatically arranged it, Jack Kerouac—as Ann Charters reports in her able biography—refused to make the ritual visit to Big Sur, notwithstanding an effusive preface Miller had written for Kerouac's *The Subterraneans*. But where besides Miller's "I just wanted to see and hear things" (*Cancer*, 260) was the formula established for Sal Paradise's "I didn't know what to say ... all I wanted to do was sneak out into the night and disappear somewhere, and go and find out what everybody was doing all over the country."[3] Similarly, what nearer precedent has the Aquarian-Age commandment to "go with the flow," motto in particular for Ken Kesey's transcontinental bus tour, than *Cancer*'s rhapsodic celebration of rivers, fluids, physical outpourings of every kind? The whole Kesey fantasy of "Edge City" as the refuge of a perilously maintained existential freedom is anticipated in *Tropic of Cancer*'s insistence (as Karl Shapiro sums it up) that where everything in America conspires to make us "lead the lives of prisoners," "the only thing for nonenslaved man to do is to move out to the edge, lose contact with the machines of organization which are as ubiquitous ... as in Russia."[4]

All this, however, may still be seen as belonging only incidentally to literary history. Where a conversational-journalistic vernacular has become more or less universal in prose, phrase-echoes inevitably abound; and echoes are not necessarily influences. Yet a book bearing with it the lurid reputation that even after twenty years of public legality still hangs about *Tropic of Cancer* is likely to leave more of an impression than it otherwise might; in such circumstances, as T. S. Eliot ruefully said of reading Edgar Allen Poe (that earlier "stumbling block for the judicial critic") in one's impressionable youth, "one cannot be sure that one's own writing has *not* been influenced."[5]

In any event, the proleptic echoes one begins to pick up in re-reading *Tropic of Cancer* do come from a broader performative field than the one so far indicated. If Miller's shudder at finding signs about syphilis and cancer posted in every Metro station (*Cancer*, 167) should remind us of Holden Caulfield's panic at discovering "Fuck you" scribbled on every wall, we are still on predictable ground. So are we, too, in catching an echo from *Tropic of Cancer* in the anthem, "Day by Day," of the rock musical *Godspell*—"The present is enough for me. Day by day," and again, "Day by day. No yesterdays and no tomorrows" (*Cancer*, 46, 135)—but what about the title, *Day by Day*, Robert Lowell gave to what became the final volume of his long verse-almanac, a collection ending, in "Epilogue," pretty much where Miller had always been: "Sometimes everything I write / ... seems a snapshot, / lurid, rapid, garish, grouped, / ... Yet why not say what happened?" In an era defining itself as essentially under siege, programs of resistance and strategies of self-preservation converge. The lines by Adrienne Rich quoted in chapter three ("I am an instrument in the shape / of a woman trying to translate pulsations / into images") have their source in the circumstances of the poem itself, which is ostensibly about the woman astronomer Caroline Herschel. But the condition of mind they speak for, far from being peculiar to latter-day feminism, is Miller's explicit starting point: "I am a sentient being stabbed by the miracle of these waters that reflect a forgotten world"; "I am a writing machine" (*Cancer*, 6, 24).

Is this true also for one of the most admired and shocking poems of the whole post-1945 period, Sylvia Plath's "Daddy"? Do the lines, "... Dachau, Auschwitz, Belsen. / I begin to talk like a Jew. / I think I may well be a Jew," look directly back to the third page of *Tropic of Cancer*: "I too would become a Jew. Why not? I already speak like a Jew. And I am ugly as a Jew"? Or are they there perhaps by way of an intermediary text, Walker Percy's *The Moviegoer* (1961):

There is nothing new in my Jewish vibrations. During the years when I had friends my Aunt Edna, who is a theosophist, noticed that all my friends were Jews. She knew why moreover: I had been a Jew in a previous incarnation. Perhaps that is it. Anyway it is true that I am Jewish by instinct. We share the same exile.

There is more than one such echo of *Tropic of Cancer* in Percy's stylish novel. "For some time now," part two, section nine, begins, "the impression has been growing upon me that everyone is dead" — "We are all alone here and we are dead," is Miller's version, in the third and concluding sentence of *Cancer*'s opening paragraph—and the last main section of *The Moviegoer* closes on an audibly Milleresque cadence: "Nothing remains but desire, and desire comes howling down Elysian Fields [the setting is New Orleans] like a mistral."[6]

For textbook literary history, though, the clinching case may prove to be Thomas Pynchon, who among other precocities was responsible for Henry Miller's first and only appearance in *The Kenyon Review*. When Pynchon's important early story, "Entropy," appeared in *Kenyon* in 1960, it sported an epigraph from page 1 of *Tropic of Cancer*:

There will be more calamities, more death, more despair. Not the slightest indication of a change anywhere.... We must get in step, a lock step, toward the prison of death. There is no escape. The weather will not change.

The passage, we note, is interestingly abridged. Pynchon, already set on his own thematic course, omitted Miller's sentences attributing these desperate conditions to "the cancer of time" and to the fact that the heroes of contemporary life have all "killed *themselves* [my emphasis] or are killing themselves."[7]

A final instance will serve to suggest that *Tropic of Cancer*'s capacity to influence began operating as soon as the book came into circulation, with consequences of unimpeachable literary seriousness. Eliot is known to have been one of *Cancer*'s first supporters and admirers[8]—to Orwell this was further proof of the book's essentially twenties character—and though the central image-motifs in Eliot's poetry commonly have a multiplicity of textual sources, those who start digging for clues in writings which Eliot made a point of commending are rarely disappointed. Rivers and oceans, Miller chants in the apocalyptic climax of *Cancer* (231–233):

... rivers that put you in touch with other men and women, with architecture, religion, plants, animals — rivers that have boats on them and in which men drown, drown not in myth and legend and books and dust of the past, but in time and space and history ... Oceans, yes! Let us have more oceans ... oceans that destroy and preserve at the same time, oceans that we can sail on, take off to new discoveries, new horizons.

And "The Dry Salvages": "Unhonoured, unpropitiated / By worshippers of the machine ... / The river is within us, the sea is all about us"; "Time the destroyer is time the preserver, / Like the river with its cargo of dead Negroes, cows and chicken coops, / ... And the ragged rock in the restless waters"; "Not fare well, / But fare forward, voyagers."[9] Of course, the confused discriminations Miller insists on in purest antinomian fashion — as between books and legends on the one hand and real people, real history, on the other — are a matter of indifference to Eliot's subtler, more knowledgeable vision. The convergence in this instance is merely in the poetry, which in both passages has the continental grandeur and freedom of American testaments generally.

All these possibilities of direct influence are of course merely speculative, at present. Moreover, most of the images and turns of phrase in question belong to a conspicuously traditional fund of idiomatic and metaphoric usage. With a writer as bookish as Miller, and bookish within fairly conventional limits, the whole matter may have to do, as much as anything, with the continuing availability of this fund for literary use. Nevertheless, the particular phrases and images I have cited come mostly from either the opening pages of *Tropic of Cancer* or its high rhetorical climaxes; and all are self-evidently central to the themes and major emphases of a book which for a quarter of a century after publication "everyone" made a point of reading—and then of reading again when it became legally available in 1961.

Notes

1. Introductory

1. John Berryman, "From the Middle and Senior Generations," *The American Scholar*, Summer 1959, rpt. in *The Freedom of the Poet* (New York: Farrar, Straus and Giroux, 1976), p. 312.
2. The references are to Ralph Waldo Emerson, "The Poet" (1841); Herman Melville, "Hawthorne and His Mosses" (1850); Walt Whitman, preface to *Leaves of Grass* (1855); Ezra Pound, letter to Harriet Monroe, 18 August 1912; Henry James, letter to Grace Norton, 14 January 1874.
3. Van Wyck Brooks, *Letters and Leadership* (New York: B. W. Huebsch, 1918), inter alia; Alfred Kazin, quoted in Sherman Paul, *Repossessing and Renewing* (Baton Rouge: Lousiana State University Press, 1976), p. 277; Norman Mailer, *Advertisements for Myself* (New York: G. P. Putnam's, 1959), p. 17.
4. I have tried to describe, at somewhat greater length, the characteristic acts of mind literature invites us to in the opening essay of my *Fictions and Events* (New York: E. P. Dutton, 1971), "The Study of Literature and the Recovery of the Historical."
5. It is that kind of activity, moreover, in which the essential character of human consciousness is most accessible as a creative force and is most regularly re-created. See Emile Durkheim, *The Elementary Forms of the Religious Life*, trans. Joseph Ward Swain (London: George Allen and Unwin, 1915), pp. 418–419, and the "Conclusion" in general.
6. Louise Bogan, "From the Journals of a Poet" (entry for 10 June 1959), *The New Yorker*, 30 January 1978, p. 48.

2. A Generation in Retreat

1. Berryman's immediate example was *The Great Gatsby*. See "F. Scott Fitzgerald," *Kenyon Review*, Winter 1946, rpt. in *The Freedom of the Poet*, p. 198.
2. Cyril Connolly, *The Unquiet Grave* (New York: Harper, 1945), p. 1; it is that elegant, sad book's opening sentence.

3. Richard Howard, *Alone with America* (New York: Atheneum, 1969), p. xi.

4. Theodore Ziolkowski, *Dimensions of the Modern Novel* (Princeton: Princeton University Press, 1969), ch. 8.

5. Critical works spelling out this assimilation of religious paradigms by secular literature are too numerous to mention here, but one recently influential study that may be cited is Frank Kermode, *The Sense of an Ending* (New York: Oxford University Press, 1967), on eschatological tracings in prose fiction. See also Professor Kermode's valuable article, "Lawrence and the Apocalyptic Types," in C. B. Cox and A. E. Dyson, eds., *Word in the Desert: The Critical Quarterly Tenth Anniversary Number* (London: Oxford University Press, 1968), pp. 14–38, and my "American Literature: Traditions and Talents," in *Fictions and Events*, pp. 157–181.

6. Sacvan Bercovitch, *The Puritan Origins of the American Self* (New Haven: Yale University Press, 1975), esp. ch. 5. In *The Imperial Self* (New York: Alfred A. Knopf, 1971) Quentin Anderson offers a more astringent view of the American cult of inflated selfhood.

7. John Berryman, "Waiting for the End, Boys," *Partisan Review*, February 1948, rpt. as "Poetry Chronicle: 1948," in *The Freedom of the Poet*, p. 308.

8. See W. Jackson Bate, *The Burden of the Past and the English Poet* (Cambridge, Massachusetts: Harvard University Press, 1970), and Harold Bloom, *The Anxiety of Influence* (New York: Oxford University Press, 1973) and *Poetry and Repression* (New Haven: Yale University Press, 1975), inter alia. One may note that Professors Bate and Bloom are themselves of the extended American generation in question: the one a year junior to Robert Lowell, the other a virtual classmate, so to speak, of Anne Sexton, Adrienne Rich, Donald Barthelme.

In both conceptual structure and general validity, these historical schemata need more searching discussion than they have yet received. (One feature that has so far escaped comment is their palpable debt to the still domineering hypothesis of Eliot's "Tradition and the Individual Talent," in relation to which, one may argue, they stand as agonistic simplifications.) Here I wish only to observe how apposite each one is, in its idea of poetic making, to the siege mentality that has settled over the whole post-1945 era, particularly where, in self-defense, the grasp of causative sequences and probabilities has become most rigidly partitioned and privatized—detached from any thoroughgoing consideration of political and societal circumstance; diminished to an essentially ad hominem framework of concern. For each of these theories factual evidence is not lacking. At the tag end of the neoclassical period, from which Professor Bate draws his central evidence, the great monuments of earlier literature could indeed be discouraging to contemplate; and in the 1940s and 1950s any number of young poets (like fledgling graduate students) both maneuvered to tap the power of their tenured elders and feared appearing too much dominated by them. In generalized form, however, both theories seem to me to speak for a radically misplaced understanding of causal priorities. The burden of the past is like the eternal silence of infinite space—a phenomenon that oppresses only insofar as the immediate facts of present life have become unmanageable, and the human space directly around us terrifies with its swarming vacuity. It is the burden of the present that paralyzes imagination.

9. Mordecai Richler, "A Sense of the Ridiculous: Paris, 1951 and After," *New American Review*, No. 4 (1968), rpt. in his *Notes on an Endangered Species* (New York: Alfred A. Knopf, 1974). There were harbingers of this change in earlier decades, of course, such as—most notably perhaps—Nathanael West's *Miss Lonelyhearts*, in 1933.

10. Allen Ginsberg, letter to Richard Eberhart, 18 May 1956, in *To Eberhart from Ginsberg* (Lincoln, Massachusetts: Penmaen Press, 1976), pp. 17-31.

11. For Lowell's recollection of these events, see "On Robert Lowell's 'Skunk Hour,'" in Anthony Ostroff, ed., *The Contemporary Poet as Artist and Critic* (Boston: Little, Brown, 1969), pp. 108-109.

12. Robert Pinsky, in *The Situation of Poetry* (Princeton: Princeton University Press, 1976), discusses this general transformation in somewhat different terms, as a change from designing poems to appear as *objects* independent of their origins to extruding them, in effect, as *statements* manneristically determined in form by the immediate circumstance of their inception.

13. Quoted by Richard Howard (in Kenneth Koch's phrasing), *Alone With America*, p. 404.

14. Gertrude Stein, "The Gradual Making of *The Making of Americans*," *Lectures in America* (New York: Random House, 1935), p. 157.

15. See Karsten Harries, "Hegel and the Future of Art," *Review of Metaphysics*, June 1974.

16. Robert Lowell, "Shifting Colors," in *Day by Day* (New York: Farrar, Straus and Giroux, 1977), p. 120.

17. Allen Ginsberg to Mark Van Doren, 19 May 1956, quoted in John Tytell, *Naked Angels: The Lives and Literature of the Beat Generation* (New York: McGraw-Hill, 1976), pp. 99–100; Jack Kerouac, "Essentials of Spontaneous Prose," *Evergreen Review*, Summer 1958, pp. 72–73.

18. Walker Percy, *The Moviegoer* (New York: Alfred A. Knopf, 1961), p. 228.

19. Fredric Jameson, "Wyndham Lewis as Futurist," *Hudson Review*, Summer 1973, pp. 325–326.

20. *American Denim: A New Folk Art*, text by Peter Beagle (New York: Harry N. Abrams, 1975), p. 132.

21. Joyce Carol Oates, *Expensive People* (New York: Vanguard Press, 1968), pp. 3–6.

22. "Saul Bellow: An Interview," *Paris Review*, No. 36 (1965), rpt. in *Writers at Work*, 3rd ser. (New York: Viking, 1967), pp. 193–194.

23. Saul Bellow, *Herzog* (New York: Viking, 1964), pp. 165–166, 341. Bellow is Bellow, of course, and Herzog, whose desperate journey concludes on this note, is a character in a novel, subject as a speaker of general truths to the usual rules of narrative irony. But it was Bellow himself who, being interviewed, closed the gap in this instance between the author's judgment and that of his character: "Any *Bildungsroman* concludes with the first step. The first *real* step" ("Saul Bellow: An Interview," p. 194).

3. Bearing Witness, Negotiating Survival

1. Norman Mailer, "Norman Mailer Versus Nine Writers," *Esquire*, July 1963, rpt. as "Some Children of the Goddess," *Cannibals and Christians* (New York: Dial Press, 1966), p. 121.

2. *All God's Dangers: The Life of Nate Shaw*, recorded and edited by Theodore Rosengarten (New York: Alfred A. Knopf, 1974).

Compare Paul Zweig, inscribing the "automythology" of his own past life: "I think I would like to write an autobiography in which there would be no people, although people would keep stumbling into it with an expression of surprise, as if they had stumbled on a shameful scene behind a bush" (*Three Journeys* [New York: Basic Books, 1976], p. 66).

3. Of his mother's mother Updike has written that though "she never to my knowledge went outside the boundaries of Pennsylvania," though she formed her more considered sentences with difficulty and was essentially uncurious and had by the end of her life almost no possessions, she had nevertheless "lived in our nation as a fish lives in the deep sea"; and he prays that his paragraphs about her may have the same natural fitness ("The Blessed Man of Boston, My Grandmother's Thimble, and Fanning Island," *Pigeon Feathers* [New York: Alfred A. Knopf, 1962], pp. 229–242).

4. *The Other America* will be remembered as the title of Michael Harrington's influential book on American poverty (1962).

5. See Tony Tanner, *City of Words* (New York: Harper and Row, 1971), p. 15: "There is an abiding dream in American literature that an unpatterned, unconditioned life is possible . . . [and] an abiding American dread that someone else is patterning your life," that "conditioning is ubiquitous."

6. Interestingly Norman Mailer in his student days wrote a play set in an insane asylum and gave it the title, "The Naked and the Dead," then tried without success to convert it into a full-scale novel (*Advertisements for Myself*, p. 27n). Clearly it was not only the title that he carried over into his best-selling war novel (1948), his first full-dress exploration of the totalitarian theme. Made over as a novel, this early work has now been published as *A Transit to Narcissus* (1978), a "Facsimile of the Original Typescript with an Introduction by the Author."

7. Kurt Vonnegut, Jr., *Cat's Cradle* (New York: Holt, Rinehart and Winston, 1963), p. 14.

8. Richard Wright's strained work in fiction during the 1950s was equally conspiracy-haunted (Williams's main character seems based on Wright). Wright, however, living in Paris at the time, was indeed a target of government surveillance and a victim of career-damaging "dirty tricks." See Michel Fabre, *The Unfinished Quest of Richard Wright*, trans. Isabel Barzun (New

York: Morrow, 1973), especially the later chapters.

9. William S. Burroughs, *Naked Lunch* (New York: Grove Press, 1966), pp. xxxix–xlii.

10. A rule anatomized by C. Wright Mills in *White Collar: The American Middle Class* (1951), where it is taken as a projection of modern work conditions, and reflected in the titles of two perceptive books by Paul Goodman during the embattled sixties: *People or Personnel* (1965) and *Like a Conquered Province* (1967).

11. For McCullers and O'Connor, as for Glasgow, there was the additional burden of a disabling physical affliction.

12. Saul Bellow, *Dangling Man* (New York: Vanguard Press, 1944), p. 126; Norman Mailer, *Why Are We in Vietnam?* (New York: G. P. Putnam's, 1967), p. 208.

13. Morris Dickstein makes roughly the same distinction, but in rather different terms. In contrast, he writes, to the big novels of the 1960s and 1970s, those of the 1950s "preserve a belief . . . in the possibilities of personal growth" and express "a Freudian faith in the maturation of self through the formation of adult relationships" ("Black Humor and History: Fiction in the Sixties," *Partisan Review*, No. 2 [1976], rpt. in *Gates of Eden* [New York: Basic Books, 1977], p. 97). That is concisely said—but not, on the face of it, entirely persuasive. Matured selves and stable adult relationships seem as rare in novels of the 1950s as they have always been in American fiction.

14. Jean-Paul Sartre, *What is Literature?*, trans. Bernard Frechtman (New York: Harper and Row, 1965), p. 51.

15. First in a notorious *Partisan Review* essay of the late 1940s ("Come Back to the Raft Ag'in, Huck Honey!" *Partisan Review*, June 1948), then more comprehensively in *Love and Death in the American Novel* (1960).

16. Eudora Welty, *The Golden Apples* (New York: Harcourt, Brace, 1949), pp. 249, 263.

17. Bellow's review is reprinted in John Hersey, ed., *Ralph Ellison: A Collection of Critical Essays* (Englewood Cliffs, New Jersey: Prentice-Hall, 1974); quotations on p. 28.

18. Edward Mendelson disagreed early on, remarking how a second reading reveals the book's "dazzling economy and coherence" ("Pynchon's Gravity," *Yale Review*, Summer 1973, p. 625). Professor Mendelson presents further arguments for the book's importance in his introduction to Edward Mendelson, ed., *Pynchon: A Collection of Critical Essays* (Englewood Cliffs,

New Jersey: Prentice-Hall, 1978). Joseph W. Slade, *Thomas Pynchon* (New York: Warner Paperback Library, 1974), offers the fullest description to date of Pynchon's fictional universe but does not really confront the possibility that it is imaginatively stillborn.

19. Tony Tanner, *City of Words*, pp. 159–161.

20. Reaching a comparable formal impasse with his comparably ambitious novel, *Degrees*, at the beginning of the 1960s, the gifted and inventive Michel Butor went over directly, in books like *Mobile*, into semiography.

21. That vision does not seem to me "complex," as has been claimed, but merely complicated, a difference worth insisting on. Roger Sale, taking a second look, has found it essentially "sentimental" ("American Fiction in 1973," *Massachusetts Review*, Autumn 1973, p. 845).

22. Roland Barthes, *The Pleasure of the Text*, trans. (very accurately) by Richard Miller (New York: Hill and Wang, 1975), pp. 17–18.

23. E. K. Bennett, *A History of the German Novelle* (London: Cambridge University Press, 1934), p. 1.

24. What is true of the single long poem or book of poems becomes true of entire careers. Irvin Ehrenpreis, reviewing a miscellany of writings in this book-length mode by poets considerably past their first youth, came recently to the glum conclusion that persistence and longevity are valued more than genuine accomplishment, and that what rates highest is simply doing a lot of work and continuing into old age ("The State of Poetry," *The New York Review of Books*, January 22, 1976).

25. Frank O'Hara, "Personism: A Manifesto," *Yügen*, No. 7 (1961), rpt. in *Standing Still and Walking in New York* (Bolinas, California: Grey Fox Press, 1975), p. 111.

26. Allen Ginsberg, letters to Mark Van Doren and John Hollander, quoted in Tytell, *Naked Angels*, pp. 100–101, 218; Frank O'Hara, "Personism: A Manifesto"; Robert Duncan, "Ideas of the Meaning of Form," *Kulchur*, No. 4 (1961); Charles Olson, "Projective Verse," *Poetry New York*, No. 3 (1950). The statements by O'Hara, Duncan, and Olson are reprinted in Donald M. Allen and Warren Tallman, eds., *The Poetics of the New American Poetry* (New York: Grove Press, 1973), pp. 353–355, 195–211, 147–158.

27. Jarrell's essays on Williams and Whitman are reprinted in

Poetry and the Age (New York: Alfred A. Knopf, 1953), pp. 215–226, 101–120.
28. A. R. Ammons, "Essay on Poetics," *Hudson Review*, Autumn 1970, p. 441.
29. Blanche Gelfant, review of Ann Charters, *Kerouac*, in *Contemporary Literature*, Summer 1974. An explanatory text for all the characteristics here described is John Barth's essay, "The Literature of Exhaustion," *Atlantic Monthly*, August 1967, rpt. in Marcus Klein, ed., *The American Novel Since World War II* (New York: Fawcett Publications, 1969). The young poet James Richardson's self-deprecating comments on his own first collection suggest that these states of mind are now being consciously appropriated for last-ditch service in preserving a role for the poet within the general dissolution. Of his poems in *Reservations* (1977) Richardson winningly remarks that they are "elegies for everything, including myself," and reflect a self "with only a tenuous grip on its surroundings." They represent an attempt "to arrest the moment long enough to say farewell, to let things go rather than be subject to their disappearance" (James Richardson, *Reservations* [Princeton: Princeton University Press, 1977], jacket copy).
30. Louis Simpson, review of James Merrill, *Divine Comedies*, *New York Times Book Review*, 21 March 1976, p. 7.
31. Quoted in Richard Howard, *Alone With America*, p. 151.
32. Helen Vendler, "False Poets and Real Poets," *New York Times Book Review*, 7 September 1975, p. 15.
33. Vendler, "False Poets and Real Poets," p. 6.

4. Old Masters: Henry Miller and Wallace Stevens

1. George Orwell, "Inside the Whale," *The Collected Essays, Journalism and Letters of George Orwell*, vol. I (New York: Harcourt, Brace and World, 1968), pp. 493–527. Orwell's remarkable essay has been widely reprinted. As for Stevens, in 1944 and 1945 alone there were notable appearances in *Kenyon Review* ("Esthétique du Mal"), in *Sewanee Review* (the lecture-essay "The Figure of the Youth as Virile Poet," and—accompanied by Hi Simons's critical study—"Description Without Place"), and in *Accent* ("The Bed of Old John Zeller" and "Less and Less Human, O Savage Spirit," in an issue also carrying Henry Miller's

brief excursus, "Let Us Be Content with Three Little Newborn Elephants"). Stevens was also cited in *Accent* (Winter 1945) as having, along with Auden and Marianne Moore, written the finest war poetry of the 1939–1945 era. In May 1947, *Partisan Review*, a fixture in Stevens's intellectual life since the late 1930s, printed "Three Academic Pieces," which he had read at Harvard during the winter.

It will round out our picture of Stevens's standing in the middle forties if we note that he was equally welcome in the poetry quarterly *Voices*. Under Harold Vinal's editorship *Voices* was a bastion of antimodernist resistance; nevertheless it devoted its Spring 1945 number to Stevens, printing not only some anthology regulars from *Harmonium* but sections of "Notes Toward a Supreme Fiction" along with several of his newest short poems.

2. The moment when Miller began writing *Tropic of Cancer*, around 1930–1931, is the same moment—according to Samuel Hynes—when for the younger English writers like Auden and Evelyn Waugh, anticipation of the war that was coming began to outweigh recollection of the war that had already occurred (*The Auden Generation* [London: Bodley Head, 1976], chs. 2, 3).

3. Orwell, "Inside the Whale," p. 520.

4. The particular reference here is to the "Anna Livia Plurabelle" installment of *Work in Progress*, the form in which *Finnegans Wake* had begun appearing in the late 1920s.

5. Orwell, "Inside the Whale," p. 498.

6. First in *The Prisoner of Sex* (1971), and then in his anthology with commentary, *Genius and Lust: A Journey Through the Major Writings of Henry Miller* (1976).

7. So Stevens, in 1948: "I have now reached an age at which I think about everything and this is a great impediment" (*Letters of Wallace Stevens*, ed. Holly Stevens [New York: Alfred A. Knopf, 1966], p. 587).

8. Orwell, "Inside the Whale," pp. 499–500.

9. The two references to Miller in Stevens's published letters say only that he hasn't read enough to have a "definite impression" of Miller—except that he is "prolix"—which was how Stevens habitually turned aside incidental requests for his opinion of important contemporaries (*Letters*, pp. 338, 772). To the right correspondent, however, Stevens can show himself entirely at ease with the knockabout hyperbole Miller regularly uses to bra-

zen out moral arguments. Writing to the mysterious J. Ronald Lane Latimer (who as much as anyone furnished Stevens the essential "impetus" to return to poetry in 1934–1935 after a decade of near silence), he offers the Milleresque comment that "selling poetry now-a-days must be very much like selling lemonade to a crowd of drunks" (*Letters,* p. 284).

10. "I think I should have difficulty putting together another volume of poems, as much as I should prefer that to a collection. But I might as well face the fact" (Stevens to Alfred A. Knopf, 22 April 1954, *Letters,* p. 829).

11. The first formulation is in the lecture, "Imagination as Value" (1948), rpt. in *The Necessary Angel: Essays on Reality and the Imagination* (New York: Alfred A. Knopf, 1951), p. 142. The second is made in the poem, "World Without Particularity," which appears to have been written between "The Auroras of Autumn" and "An Ordinary Evening in New Haven," also during 1948.

12. Northrop Frye, "The Realistic Oriole," *Hudson Review,* Autumn 1957, rpt. in *Fables of Identity* (New York: Harcourt, Brace and World, 1963), p. 255.

13. Schwartz's comment is in "Wallace Stevens: An Appreciation," *New Republic,* 22 August 1955, rpt. in *Selected Essays of Delmore Schwartz* (Chicago: University of Chicago Press, 1970), p. 195. The Stevens phrases quoted here are from "An Ordinary Evening in New Haven," xxxi (1949), and "The Well-Dressed Man With a Beard" (1941), one of four poems alluded to in the retrospective self-querying of "As You Leave the Room" (1947; 1955).

14. *Letters,* p. 501.

15. John Berryman, *The Dream Songs* (New York: Farrar, Straus and Giroux, 1969). No. 219 ("So Long? Stevens").

16. The several allusions here, easily substantiated in Thomas F. Walsh, *Concordance to the Poetry of Wallace Stevens* (University Park, Pennsylvania: Pennsylvania State University Press, 1963), are to "Sunday Morning," "Notes Toward a Supreme Fiction," "Of Ideal Time and Choice," "The Owl in the Sarcophagus," "The Plain Sense of Things," "Esthétique du Mal," "Credences of Summer," and "The Rock."

17. "An Ordinary Evening in New Haven," xii.

18. Frank Kermode, *Wallace Stevens* (Edinburgh: Oliver and

Boyd, 1960), pp. 20-21. The *Adagia* entry is in Wallace Stevens, *Opus Posthumous*, ed. Samuel French Morse (New York: Alfred A. Knopf, 1957), p. 158.

19. Not only icy polar auroras project this terror. From some points of view it is preeminently "the human" that is "alien" ("Less and Less Human, O Savage Spirit").

20. Helen Vendler, *On Extended Wings: Wallace Stevens' Longer Poems* (Cambridge, Massachusetts: Harvard University Press, 1969), p. 50.

21. Kermode, *Wallace Stevens*, p. 6.

22. "The Woman That Had More Babies Than That" (1939).

23. This corresponds to the theme of "myself and the world" which Faulkner in his later years mistakenly identified as the single source of his own narrative power (Faulkner to Malcolm Cowley, November 1944, in Malcolm Cowley, ed., *The Faulkner-Cowley File* [New York: Viking Press, 1966], p. 14).

24. *Letters*, p. 454.

25. Holly Stevens, *Souvenirs and Prophecies: The Young Wallace Stevens* (New York: Alfred A. Knopf, 1977), p. 4.

26. *Letters*, p. 71.

27. *Letters*, p. 89. "Personality must be kept secret before the world," he had decided during his first New York summer, looking back with distaste on that force-fed Harvard College "subjectivity"—his word—which may also have been the institutional irritant that impelled Eliot, a decade later, toward the famous doctrine of poetic impersonality (*Letters*, p. 44).

28. *Letters*, p. 86.

29. Quoted in *Souvenirs and Prophecies*, p. 70.

30. *Souvenirs and Prophecies*, p. 137.

31. The few letters so far available from the years 1924 to 1930 offer next to nothing in the way of clues, even though they are mostly replies to inquiries about new poems or commentaries on old ones. See *Letters*, pp. 241-258.

32. "Notes Toward a Supreme Fiction," I, iv.

33. *Letters*, p. 602. Holly Stevens's recollections of domestic circumstance are in *Letters*, pp. 242-243, 255-256, 450n. Writing to Archibald MacLeish of his unwillingness to assume the Norton chair in poetry at Harvard for 1955-1956, Stevens explained that an extended absence from his firm at the age of seventy-five might "precipitate the retirement that I want so much to put off.

What is more I cannot imagine taking up the routine of the office again, at my age, after being away from it for a long period of time. These considerations, and others, leave me no choice" (*Letters*, p. 853).

34. *Letters*, p. 620.

35. "An Ordinary Evening in New Haven," xxviii; again, my emphasis.

36. Did this have anything to do with their common Germanness? One needs to be tentative about the mysteries of American ethnicity and acculturation, and in any case Stevens was only partly Pennsylvania-German (and preferred to think of himself as "Holland Dutch"). The relatively undisturbed insulation of the Pennsylvania German communities, however, is a palpable historical fact, traces of which persist deep into the electronic and superhighway era; and fifteen years of living in their neighborhood have left me persuaded that the odd custom of Stevens's personal life derives in some part from the custom of the country in and around Reading, Pennsylvania. Certain peculiarities of Stevens's verse idiom may also be in question here. "Personally," he wrote Henry Church in 1939, "I like words to sound wrong" (*Letters*, p. 340). Where better than in the heart of Berks County could he have acquired that predilection? As for Miller there is his own recollection: "Until I went to school I spoke nothing but German and the atmosphere in which I was raised, despite the fact that my parents were born in America, was German through and through" ("Biographical Note," *The Cosmological Eye* [Norfolk, Connecticut: New Directions, 1941], p. 357). And there is Karl Shapiro's fine comment: "In certain ways he is quite German. I have often thought that the Germans make the best Americans, though they certainly make the worst Germans" ("The Greatest Living Author," introduction to *Tropic of Cancer* [New York: Grove Press, 1961], p. vii).

37. For Kenner's minority report on Stevens, see *A Homemade World: The American Modernist Writers* (New York: Alfred A. Knopf, 1975), pp. 50–57, 67–85.

5. Prospects

1. To Thankmar Freiherr von Münchausen, 6 March 1915. Quotations from Rilke's letters of 1914–1918 are from *Wartime Letters of Rainier Maria Rilke*, trans. M. D. Herter Nor-

ton (New York: W. W. Norton, 1940). I have here and there modified these translations for greater clarity and literalness. For the original texts see Rainier Maria Rilke, *Briefe aus den Jahren 1914 bis 1921* (Leipzig: Insel-Verlag, 1937).

2. To Helene von Nostitz, 12 July 1915.

3. To Bernhard von der Marwitz, 12 February 1918. So too Paul Klee, his years at the Bauhaus behind him, at the end of the aphoristic treatise on modern art he delivered at Jena in 1924:

Sometimes I dream of a work of really great breadth, ranging through the whole region of element, object, meaning and style.

... [But] nothing can be rushed. It must grow, it should grow of itself, and if the time ever comes for that work—then so much the better!

We must go on seeking it! We have found parts, but not the whole! We still lack the ultimate power, for: no multitude supports us.

But we seek a people. We began over there in the Bauhaus. We began there with a community to which each one of us gave what he had. More we cannot do.

(Paul Klee, *On Modern Art*, trans. Paul Findlay [London: Faber and Faber, 1948], pp. 54–55)

4. Paul Fussell develops a comparable argument in impressive detail as regards the literature of the last half century in *The Great War and Modern Memory* (1975). My friendly amendment here is simply to observe that it did not require frontline experience to sense, as early as 1915, the enormity of what was taking place.

To Rilke as to Proust, too, in the superb wartime passages of *Le Temps retrouvé* (and in a comparable way to Randolph Bourne, in certain *Seven Arts* essays of 1917), the first symptom of cultural breakdown was the corruption of literary and intellectual integrity by the war spirit, through a time-serving journalism that systematically transformed the realities of the moment into a pseudo-reality of news reports. See, inter alia, the letter to Bernhard von der Marwitz, 9 March 1918.

5. Students of political history describe a corresponding development in the sphere of popular agitation: a measurable retreat of movements of dissidence and reform from the established centers of population and power. George Rudé, reviewing John Stevenson, ed., *London in the Age of Reform*, remarks of the

Queen Caroline affair of the 1820s that "it was the last time that the City of London set the pace in a popular national movement" (*Times Literary Supplement*, 9 December 1977, p. 1453).
6. Emerson summarizes this exchange in *English Traits*, ch. xvi.
7. For an extended discussion see David Noble, *America by Design: Science, Technology, and the Rise of Corporate Capitalism* (New York: Alfred A. Knopf, 1977), chs. 8–9.
8. Stanley Kunitz, "The Sense of a Life: A Memoir," *The New York Times Book Review*, 16 October 1977, p. 34.
9. Harold Rosenberg, "Twenty Years of Jasper Johns," *The New Yorker*, 26 December 1977, p. 42.
10. Kunitz, "The Sense of a Life," p. 34.
11. See Peter Jones, *Philosophy and the Novel* (Oxford: Clarendon Press, 1975), p. 188 and passim.

Coda: A Note on the Influence of *Tropic of Cancer*

1. Norman Mailer, *Genius and Lust: A Journey Through the Major Writings of Henry Miller* (New York: Grove Press, 1976), pp. 2–4.
2. Quoted by Karl Shapiro, "The Greatest Living Author," p. xviii.
3. Jack Kerouac, *On the Road* (New York: Viking Press, 1957), p. 67.
4. Karl Shapiro, "The Greatest Living Author," p. xx. The bus tour of Kesey's Merry Pranksters is described in Tom Wolfe, *The Electric Kool-Aid Acid Test* (1968).
5. T. S. Eliot, "From Poe to Valéry" (1948), rpt. in *To Criticize the Critic* (New York: Farrar, Straus and Giroux, 1965), p. 27.
6. Walker Percy, *The Moviegoer*, pp. 88–89, 99, 228.
7. The "edge" metaphor, too, turns up in Pynchon, though now as a place of indeterminate terror; the "Zone" is "the new edge," we learn in *Gravity's Rainbow* (New York: Viking Press, 1973), pp. 722–723.
8. *Tropic of Cancer* received a favorable notice in *Criterion*, October 1935, as part of Montgomery Belgion's "French Chronicle," where it is called the most interesting new book of the Paris season: "The astounding thing is that the novel has qualities almost as great as its defects. There is no plot, but there is a pattern." There is also "a marked distinction in the writing,"

and, above all, a "dynamism" (p. 86). *Black Spring* was reviewed sympathetically in the April 1937 *Criterion* by A. Desmond Hawkins, who praised—"when Mr. Miller is not imitating other authors"—"the freshness of its idiom," describing this quality in thoroughly Eliotesque fashion: "This Paris-American idiom, loose and fragmentary as it may be, is the one impersonal contribution to imaginative prose style in our time" (p. 503). In October 1937, Miller himself appeared as a *Criterion* author, with a review-article on Anaïs Nin and diary literature. A second and last contribution of Miller's was carried in the final number of *Criterion*, in January of 1939. It is a review of Erich Gutkind, *The Absolute Collective: A Philosophical Attempt to Overcome Our Broken State*, and it is printed just ahead of Eliot's own valedictory as editor.

9. T. S. Eliot, *Four Quartets* (New York: Harcourt, Brace, 1943), pp. 21, 24, 26.

Index

Accent: A Quarterly of New Literature, 186–187n
Adams, Henry, 71n, 160
Adler, Renata, 163; Speedboat, 17
Agee, James, 54
Aiken, Conrad: Blue Voyage, 16
Albee, Edward: The American Dream, 58–59
All God's Dangers: The Life of Nate Shaw, 48–50, 166
All the Sad Young Men (F. Scott Fitzgerald), 16
American Denim: A New Folk Art, 44
An American Tragedy (Theodore Dreiser), 16, 39
Amherst College, 34
Ammons, A. R., 82; "Essay on Poetics," 92, 98; Sphere, 79, 85, 94; Tape for the Turn of the Year, 79, 94
Anderson, Quentin: The Imperial Self, 180n
Anderson, Sherwood: Dark Laughter, 16; A Story-Teller's Story, 16
Apollinaire, Guillaume, 84; as poetic influence, 33
archy and mehitabel (Don Marquis), 16
Ardrey, Robert: The Territorial Imperative, 71–72n
Arnold, Matthew, 43n
Arrowsmith (Sinclair Lewis), 16
Ashbery, John, 36, 82; Self-Portrait in a Convex Mirror, 18

Auden, W. H., 20, 159n, 187n; as poetic influence, 29, 81; as war poet, 187n; "In Memory of W. B. Yeats," 80–81, 99; "1929," 18

Bakhtin, Mikhail, 157n
Baldwin, James: Go Tell It on the Mountain, 77n
Baraka, Amiri (LeRoi Jones), 65n
Barren Ground (Ellen Glasgow), 16
Barth, John: The End of the Road, 64–65; Giles Goat-Boy, 58; "The Literature of Exhaustion," 186n
Barthelme, Donald, 37, 160, 163, 180n; Amateurs, 18; The Dead Father, 18
Barthes, Roland: Le Plaisir du texte, 76
Bate, W. Jackson: The Burden of the Past and the English Poet, 31–32, 180–181n
Baudelaire, Charles, 111; Le Spleen de Paris, 43n
Bayley, John: on W. S. Merwin, 93
Beach, Joseph Warren: American Fiction: 1920–1940, 28
Beagle, Peter S., 44
Beckett, Samuel, 39, 159n; Imagination Dead! Imagine, 37; Lessness, 37
Behrman, S. N.: The Second Man, 16
Belgion, Montgomery: on Tropic of Cancer, 192–193n

Bellow, Saul, 39, 45–46, 171; on universities, 161–162n; review of *Invisible Man*, 68–69; *The Adventures of Augie March*, 116, 170–171; *Dangling Man*, 63; *Henderson the Rain King*, 64–65, 77n; *Herzog*, 45–46, 52, 182n; *Humboldt's Gift*, 17; *Seize the Day*, 64–65, 77n; *To Jerusalem and Back*, 152; *The Victim*, 62–63

Benjamin, Walter: on the journal as literary form, 95, 95n; "The Work of Art in the Age of Mechanical Reproduction," 101n

Bennett, E. K.: on the novella, 77

Bercovitch, Sacvan: *The Puritan Origins of the American Self*, 26

Berger, Thomas: *Who Is Teddy Villanova?*, 17

Bernanos, Georges, 54

Berryman, John, 4–5, 30, 38, 160; on masterpieces, 19; on Robert Lowell, 30; *Berryman's Sonnets*, 34; *Delusions, Etc.*, 38; *The Dream Songs*, 19, 34, 91, 99; *Homage to Mistress Bradstreet*, 34; *Love & Fame*, 38, 94; "So Long? Stevens," 136, 142

Bishop, Elizabeth, 82n; "Argument," 103; *Geography III*, 18

Black Boy (Richard Wright), 15

Black Mountain College, 83, 85, 93

Blake, William, 159n; "To the Muses," 37

Bloom, Harold: on Wallace Stevens, 108n, 143–144n, 151; *The Anxiety of Influence*, 31–32; *Poetry and Repression*, 180–181n

Blue Voyage (Conrad Aiken), 16

Bly, Robert, 37, 82

Bogan, Louise, 13, 29

Bourne, Randolph, 191n

Brautigan, Richard, 37

Bread Loaf Writers' Conference, 29

Bridges, Robert, 159n

Bromwich, David: on A. R. Ammons, 79

Brooks, Gwendolyn, 82n

Brooks, Van Wyck, 5–6, 16

Brown, Merle E.: on Wallace Stevens, 143n

Brown, Norman O.: influence on Thomas Pynchon, 74n; *Love's Body*, 71–72n

Buffalo Springfield, The: "For What It's Worth," 56, 78

Burke, Kenneth, 66n

Burroughs, William S.: *Naked Lunch*, 60–61, 170

Butor, Michel, 20; *Degrees*, 185n; *Mobile*, 185n

Byron, George Gordon, Lord, 159n

Camus, Albert, 124n

Candy (Terry Southern and Mason Hoffenberg), 33

Cane (Jean Toomer), 16

Capote, Truman: *In Cold Blood*, 53n

Carlyle, Thomas, 41, 159

Cather, Willa, 62, 160; *The Professor's House*, 16

Cézanne, Paul, 154, 154n

Charters, Ann: *Kerouac*, 172, 186n

Cheever, John: *Falconer*, 17

Chicago, University of, 68

Church, Barbara, 148

Church, Henry, 190n

City Lights Bookstore (San Francisco), 172

Clifton, Lucille, 92

Coleridge, Samuel Taylor, 159n

Coles, Robert, 52–55

Collins, William: "Ode on the Poetical Character," 37

Columbia College, 33, 34, 68, 94

Commentary, 68

Composition as Explanation (Gertrude Stein), 16

Connolly, Cyril: *The Unquiet Grave*, 20

Conroy, Frank: *Stop-Time*, 116

Index

Cooper, James Fenimore, 160
Coover, Robert: *The Public Burning*, 18
Cornell University, 85
Cortazar, Julio, 20n
Craig's Wife (George Kelly), 16
Crane, Hart, 143n, 144; as poetic influence, 84–85; "Voyages," 143n; *White Buildings*, 16
Crane, Stephen, 160
Creeley, Robert, 38n, 82, 100
The Criterion, 192–193n
Cummings, E. E., 16, 30, 150, 160; *The Enormous Room*, 16; "now does our world descend," 31

Dark Laughter (Sherwood Anderson), 16
Davie, Donald: on Robert Lowell, 94
The Dial, 147
Dickens, Charles, 159n
Dickinson, Emily, 104n, 160
Dickey, James, 39
Dickey, William, 82, 93
Dickstein, Morris: *Gates of Eden*, 184n
Diderot, Denis: *Rameau's Nephew*, 51
Doctorow, E. L.: *Ragtime*, 17, 70
Doctor Zhivago (Boris Pasternak), 51
Donnelly, Ignatius: *Caesar's Column*, 57
Dorn, Edward: *Gunslinger*, 79
Dos Passos, John, 160; *Manhattan Transfer*, 16
Dostoevsky, Fyodor: *Notes From Underground*, 28
A Draft of XVI Cantos (Ezra Pound), 16
Dreiser, Theodore, 28, 51, 112, 160; *An American Tragedy*, 16, 39; *Jennie Gerhardt*, 49
Dugan, Alan, 82
Duncan, Robert, 84n; "Ideas of the Meaning of Form," 47, 83–84
Durkheim, Emile: *The Elementary Forms of the Religious Life*, 10, 11n, 179n
Durrell, Lawrence, 170
Dylan, Bob: "Mr. Tambourine Man," 171

Eberhart, Richard, 88n
Ehrenpreis, Irvin: "The State of Poetry," 185n
Eliot, T. S., 3, 30, 36, 86, 108, 108n, 133, 144, 147n, 158–159, 159n, 160, 175–176, 189n, 193n; as literary influence, 29; on Poe, 173; "The Dry Salvages," 176; *Four Quartets*, 15, 35n; *The Hollow Men*, 16; *Homage to John Dryden*, 16; "The Love Song of J. Alfred Prufrock," 26; *Sweeney Agonistes*, 16, 36; "Tradition and the Individual Talent," 86, 180n; "The Waste Land," 19, 35n, 86
Ellison, Ralph, 28, 101; *Invisible Man*, 61–62, 64–65, 68–69, 77n
Ellman, Mary: *Thinking About Women*, 128
Ellman, Richard, 2n
Emerson, Ralph Waldo, 4, 5, 7, 69, 107, 116, 158–159, 160; on *Leaves of Grass*, 7, 65; *English Traits*, 192n; *Nature*, 125–126; "The Poet," 5, 100
The Enormous Room (E. E. Cummings), 16–17

Fabre, Michel: *The Unfinished Quest of Richard Wright*, 183–184n
Farrell, James T., 51
Faulkner, William, 2–3, 75, 108, 147n, 158, 159n, 163, 189n; *Go Down Moses*, 15; *The Hamlet*, 15; *Mosquitoes*, 16; *Soldier's Pay*, 16; *The Sound and the Fury*, 26; *The Wild Palms*, 65
Feldman, Irving, 82
Ferlinghetti, Lawrence, 172
Fiedler, Leslie: *Love and Death in the American Novel*, 67, 184n
Fielding, Henry, 159n
Finkel, Donald: *Adequate Earth*, 79

Fitzgerald, F.Scott: *All the Sad Young Men*, 16; *The Great Gatsby*, 16, 39, 49, 65
Fleming, Ian, 75
Forster, E. M., 20, 159n
For Whom the Bell Tolls (Ernest Hemingway), 15
Four Quartets, (T. S. Eliot), 15
Fox, Paula: *The Widow's Children*, 18
Fox, Robin, 71–72n
Frankfurt Institute of Social Research, 43n
Freud, Sigmund, 128
Frost, Robert, 30, 108n, 159, 160; as literary influence, 29
Frye, Northrop: on Wallace Stevens, 133–134
Fuentes, Carlos, 20n
Fussell, Edwin, 96–97
Fussell, Paul: *The Great War and Modern Memory*, 191n

Gaddis, William: *JR*, 17; *The Recognitions*, 39
García Marquez, Gabriel, 20n
Gardner, John: *October Light*, 17
Garrigue, Jean, 30, 82n
Gass, William H.: *On Being Blue*, 18; "The Pedersen Kid," 77n
Gelfant, Blanche: on Jack Kerouac, 93
Gentlemen Prefer Blondes (Anita Loos), 16
Gide, André: *Les Faux-monnayeurs*, 166n
Ginsberg, Allen, 33–34, 39, 82, 83–84, 88n, 91, 94, 99, 101, 115n, 160, 163; on "Howl," 88n; "America," 104; *Howl*, 33, 171
Glasgow, Ellen, 62, 184n; *Barren Ground*, 16
Go Down Moses (William Faulkner), 15
Godspell, 173
Goethe, Johann Wolfgang: *Elective Affinities*, 95
Goodman, Paul: *Like a Conquered Province*, 184n; *People or Personnel*, 184n
Gotham Book Mart (New York), 29
Grass, Günter, 20
Graves, Robert, 159n
Gray, Thomas: "The Progress of Poesy," 37
The Great Gatsby (F. Scott Fitzgerald), 16, 39, 49, 65
The Great God Brown (Eugene O'Neill), 15
Greimas, A. J., 66n
Grolier Book Shop (Cambridge, Mass.), 29

The Hamlet (William Faulkner), 15
Hardy, Thomas, 159n
Harmonium (Wallace Stevens), 16, 131, 147
Harries, Karsten: "Hegel and the Future of Art," 182n
Harrington, Michael: *The Other America*, 183n
Hartigan, Grace, 33
Harvard College, 68, 187n, 189n
Hawkes, John: *Travesty*, 17
Hawkins, A. Desmond: on *Black Spring*, 193n
Hawthorne, Nathaniel, 19, 160
Hecht, Anthony, 82
Hegel, Georg Wilhelm Friedrich, 37, 182n
Heller, Joseph, 39; *Catch-22*, 38, 58, 58n, 113–114, 114n; *Something Happened*, 39
Hemingway, Ernest, 28, 29, 113, 129n, 160; as literary influence, 37; *A Farewell to Arms*, 28; *For Whom the Bell Tolls*, 15; *In Our Time*, 16; *Men Without Women*, 16; *The Sun Also Rises*, 16
Heyward, DuBose: *Porgy*, 16
Hoffman, Daniel, 82
Hofstadter, Richard: *The Paranoid Style in American Politics*, 64
The Hollow Men (T. S. Eliot), 16
Homage to John Dryden (T. S. Eliot), 16

Index

Hoover, Herbert, 49
Housman, A. E., 159n
Howard, Richard: *Alone with America*, 21
How to Write Short Stories (Ring Lardner), 16
Hughes, Langston, 65n
Hugo, Richard, 82; *What Thou Lovest Well Remains American*, 18
Hynes, Samuel: *The Auden Generation*, 187n

The Iceman Cometh (Eugene O'Neill), 15
In the American Grain (William Carlos Williams), 16
In Our Time (Ernest Hemingway), 16
International Labor Defense Committee, 49

James, Henry, 5, 133, 159, 160; "The Future of the Novel," 152; *The Princess Casamassima*, 57n
James, William, 141, 160; *The Varieties of Religious Experience*, 23
Jameson, Fredric, 42–43, 43n, 47–48
Jarrell, Randall, 30; on Walt Whitman, 85; on William Carlos Williams, 85; *The Lost World*, 34–35; *Poetry and the Age*, 185–186n
Jeffers, Robinson, 97, 150; *Tamar and Other Poems*, 16
Jewett, Sarah Orne, 160
Johnson, Samuel, 159n
Jones, Peter: *Philosophy and the Novel*, 168
Jong, Erica: *Fear of Flying*, 170
Joyce, James, 20, 54, 110–111, 159n; *Finnegans Wake*, 132, 187n; *Ulysses*, 26, 115n, 169

Kafka, Franz: as literary influence, 63
Kazin, Alfred, 6

Keats, John, 88n, 157n, 159n; letters, 84n
Kees, Weldon, 30
Keithley, George: *The Donner Party*, 79
Kelly, George: *Craig's Wife*, 16
Kelly, Robert: *The Common Shore*, 79
Kennedy, John F., 75
Kenner, Hugh: on Wallace Stevens, 151
Kenyon College, 29, 34, 35, 68, 85
The Kenyon Review, 35, 175, 186n
Kermode, Frank: on Wallace Stevens, 137–139, 139n; *The Sense of an Ending*, 180n
Kerouac, Jack, 92; and Henry Miller, 172; on hipsters, 65–66n; "Essentials of Spontaneous Prose," 39; *On the Road*, 33, 64–65, 67, 172; *The Subterraneans*, 172
Kerouac, John E. (Jack Kerouac): *The Town and the City*, 33
Kesey, Ken, 172; *One Flew over the Cuckoo's Nest*, 58
Kessler, Jascha, 91
Kingston, Maxine Hong: *The Woman Warrior*, 18
Klee, Paul: *On Modern Art*, 191n
Knight, Etheridge, 101; "Titanic" toast, 69
Knopf, Alfred A., 131
Koch, Kenneth, 82, 181n
Kunitz, Stanley: on Robert Lowell, 163–165

Lardner, Ring: *How to Write Short Stories*, 16
Lawrence, D. H., 20, 159n; *Lady Chatterley's Lover*, 169
Leaves of Grass (Walt Whitman), 7
Levertov, Denise, 92
Levine, Philip, 82
Lewis, Oscar: *La Vida*, 53n
Lewis, Sinclair: *Arrowsmith*, 16; *Babbitt*, 19
London, Jack, 160; *The Iron Heel*, 57

Loos, Anita: *Gentlemen Prefer Blondes*, 16
Lorca, Federico García, 84
Lorenz, Konrad: *On Aggression*, 71–72n
Lovecraft, H. P.: as subliterary influence, 56
Lowell, Robert, 15, 30, 33–34, 94–95, 160, 163–165, 180n; on Mallarmé, 37; *Day by Day*, 18, 173; "For the Union Dead," 95; *History*, 38, 79, 91, 165; *Life Studies*, 34, 91, 94–95; *Lord Weary's Castle*, 30; *Notebook*, 19, 95, 165; "Words for Hart Crane," 85

McConkey, James; *Crossroads*, 116
McCullers, Carson, 62, 184n; "The Ballad of the Sad Café," 77n
MacLeish, Archibald, 189n
MacNeice, Louis, 29
The Magic Christian (Terry Southern), 33
Mailer, Norman, 4, 6, 28, 41, 170–171; on Henry Miller, 120, 170–171; on John Updike, 48; *An American Dream*, 59, 116; *The Armies of the Night*, 19, 53n, 166–167; "The Naked and the Dead," 183n; *The Naked and the Dead*, 183n; *A Transit to Narcissus*, 183n; *Why Are We in Vietnam?*, 19, 63, 77n, 170
The Making of Americans (Gertrude Stein), 16
Malamud, Bernard: *The Assistant*, 77n
Malcolm X (Malcolm Little): *The Autobiography of Malcolm X*, 166–167
Mallarmé, Stéphane, 37
Manhattan Transfer (John Dos Passos), 16
Mariani, Paul, 93
Marquis, Don: *archy and mehitabel*, 16

Matisse, Henri, 110–111
Matthiessen, F. O., 2n
Melville, Herman, 75, 160; "Bartleby the Scrivener," 65; "Hawthorne and His Mosses," 5
Mendelson, Edward: on *Gravity's Rainbow*, 184–185n
Men Without Women (Ernest Hemingway), 16
Meredith, William: on A. R. Ammons, 94
Merrill, James, 82; "The Book of Ephraim," 40, 79; *Divine Comedies*, 18; "An Urban Convalescence," 103
Merwin, W. S., 82, 93
Middlebrook, Diane: on Allen Ginsberg, 101
Miles, Josephine, 82n
Miller, Henry, 107–133, 149–150, 154; as literary influence, 29, 169–177; contributions to *Criterion*, 193n; his Germanness, 189n; *Black Spring*, 109, 193n; *The Colossus of Maroussi*, 109; "Let Us Be Content with Three Little New-Born Elephants," 186–187n; *Tropic of Cancer*, 106, 108n, 109–133, 169–177, 187n
Miller, Vassar, 82
Mills, C. Wright: *White Collar*, 184n
Milton, John, 91, 92, 159n
Moore, Marianne, 30, 84; as literary influence, 29; as war poet, 187n; review of *Harmonium*, 147; *Observations*, 16; "Poetry," 36
Morris, John V.: on Adrienne Rich, 80–81
Morris, Wright: *The Deep Sleep*, 77n; *Love Among the Cannibals*, 64–65
Mosquitoes (William Faulkner), 16
A Mother's Recompense (Edith Wharton), 16
Mottram, Eric: on Denise

Levertov, 92; on Diane Wakoski, 92
Musil, Robert: *The Man Without Qualities*, 22–23

Nabokov, Vladimir: *Bend Sinister*, 77n; *Details of a Sunset and Other Stories*, 17; *Lolita*, 77n; *Pale Fire*, 59; *Pnin*, 77n
Nate Shaw (pseud.): *All God's Dangers*, 48–50, 166–167
Native Son (Richard Wright), 15
Newbegin's bookstore (San Francisco), 29
The New Oxford Book of American Verse, 2
The New York Review of Books, 94
The New Yorker, 29, 163
Nietzsche, Friedrich, 126, 132; as literary influence, 37
Nin, Anaïs, 169, 193n
Noble, David: *America by Design: Science, Technology, and the Rise of Corporate Capitalism*, 192n
Notes Toward a Supreme Fiction (Wallace Stevens), 15

Oates, Joyce Carol, 51–55; *The Assassins*, 17; *Crossing the Border*, 17; *Expensive People*, 44; *them*, 51–52
Observations (Marianne Moore), 16
O'Connor, Flannery, 62, 184n; *Wise Blood*, 77n
O'Hara, Frank, 33, 36, 82, 84n, 94, 99, 164–165; "The Day Lady Died," 103–104; *Lunch Poems*, 33; "Personism," 80, 83–84
Olson, Charles, 30, 84n; as poetic influence, 78–79; *The Maximus Poems*, 79; "Projective Verse," 83–84
O'Neill, Eugene: *The Great God Brown*, 16; *The Iceman Cometh*, 15
Oppen, George, 38n
Orwell, George: "Inside the Whale" (on Henry Miller), 107–108, 109–110, 112, 115, 169, 175; *1984*, 63
The Oxford Book of American Verse, 2

Parnassus: Poetry in Review, 89–101
Partisan Review, 184n, 187n
Pasternak, Boris: *Doctor Zhivago*, 51
Paul (Saint): epistle to the Philippians, 24
Paul, Sherman, 179n
Paz, Octavio: "A Literature Without Criticism," 20n
Percy, Walker: *Lancelot*, 18; *The Moviegoer*, 40, 77n, 174–175
Piaget, Jean, 10, 51
Picasso, Pablo, 29
Pinsky, Robert: "Essay on Psychiatrists," 18; "Sadness and Happiness," 105; *The Situation of Poetry*, 181n
Pirsig, Robert M.: *Zen and the Art of Motorcycle Maintenance*, 116, 166–167
Plath, Sylvia, 30, 82, 99; "Daddy," 174; "Elm," 104
Poe, Edgar Allan, 4, 38, 111, 158, 159n, 160; "Marginalia," 116
Poetry Now, 89
Pope, Alexander, 159n
Porgy (DuBose Heyward), 16
Port of New York (Paul Rosenfeld), 16
Pound, Ezra, 3, 5, 16, 30, 35n, 97, 108n, 159; as poetic influence, 78–79, 81; as teacher, 29, 84; *The Cantos*, 31, 78–79, 132; *A Draft of XVI Cantos*, 16
The Professor's House (Willa Cather), 16
Proust, Marcel: *A la recherche du temps perdu*, 110; *Le Temps retrouvé*, 191n
Pynchon, Thomas, 39; *The Crying of Lot 49*, 43n, 77–78, 77n; "Entropy," 175; *Gravity's Rainbow*, 70–76, 81, 192n; *V.*, 70–72

Rameau's Nephew (Denis Diderot), 51
Ransom, John Crowe, 85; as teacher, 29
Reed, Ishmael, 101; *Flight to Canada*, 18
Reverdy, Pierre: as poetic influence, 33
Rexroth, Kenneth: as literary influence, 29
Rich, Adrienne, 53–55, 80–81, 82, 92, 160, 180n; *Of Woman Born*, 18; "Planetarium," 81, 174
Richardson, James: *Reservations*, 186n
Richler, Mordecai: on American humour noir, 32–33, 56
Rilke, Rainer Maria, 85; wartime letters, 152–157, 191n
Rimbaud, Arthur: as literary influence, 37
Rivers, Larry, 33
Robbins, Tom: *Even Cowgirls Get the Blues*, 18
Roberts, Elizabeth Madox: *The Time of Man*, 16
Roethke, Theodore, 30
Rosenberg, Harold, 164; *The Tradition of the New*, 27n
Rosenfeld, Paul: *Port of New York*, 16
Roth, Philip: *Portnoy's Complaint*, 170; *The Professor of Desire*, 17; *Reading Myself and Others*, 17
Rudé, George, 191–192n

Sale, Roger: on the American imperial novel, 75; on *Gravity's Rainbow*, 75, 185n
Salinger, J. D.: *The Catcher in the Rye*, 62, 64, 77n, 116, 173
San Francisco: as literary center, 29, 33–34, 85
Santayana, George, 141
Sartre, Jean-Paul: *What Is Literature?*, 66–67
Schwartz, Delmore, 30; on Wallace Stevens, 134; *Summer Knowledge*, 35; *The World Is a Wedding*, 37–38

Scott, Walter, 159n
The Second Man (S. N. Behrman), 16
Segal, Clancy: *Zone of the Interior*, 17
The Sewanee Review, 35, 186n
Sexton, Anne, 30, 100–101, 180n
Shakespeare & Company (Paris), 29
Shapiro, Karl: on Henry Miller, 108n, 190n; on *Tropic of Cancer*, 172
Shaw, George Bernard, 159n
Simons, Hi: on Wallace Stevens, 186n
Simpson, Louis, 82, 93
Sissman, L. E., 82
Skinner, B. F.: *Beyond Freedom and Dignity*, 71–72
Slade, Joseph W.: *Thomas Pynchon*, 185n
Slavitt, David: *Vital Signs*, 39
Smart, Christopher, 84
Snodgrass, W. D., 82; *Heart's Needle*, 35, 91
Snyder, Gary, 97–98, 100, 163; *Regarding Wave*, 97; "Smokey the Bear Sutra," 104–105; "What you should know to be a Poet," 97–98, 98n
Soldier's Pay (William Faulkner), 16
Southern, Terry: *Candy* (with Mason Hoffenberg), 33; *The Magic Christian*, 33
Spring and All (William Carlos Williams), 16
Stein, Gertrude, 36; *Composition as Explanation*, 16; *The Making of Americans*, 16, 36–37
Steinbeck, John, 111
Stendhal, 19
Stevens, Elsie Kachel, 146–148
Stevens, Holly, 144–146, 146n, 148
Stevens, Wallace, 15, 16, 30, 31, 35n, 87, 107–109, 113, 118, 129–151, 154; as Pennsylvanian, 190n; as poetic influence, 29, 81; as war poet, 187n; early

journals, 144–146; his Germanness, 190n; late poems, 87, 129; on Henry Miller, 187n; "Adagia," 138; *The Auroras of Autumn*, 31, 188n; "Chocorua to Its Neighbor," 137; *Collected Poems*, 130n, 131ff; "Effects of Analogy," 131; "Esthétique du Mal," 108, 137, 141–143, 186n; *Harmonium*, 16, 131, 147; "Imagination as Value," 133; "The Man with the Blue Guitar," 113, 132; "The Noble Rider and the Sound of Words," 149–150; *Notes Toward a Supreme Fiction*, 15; "Notes Toward a Supreme Fiction," 15, 108, 132, 136, 138, 143n, 147, 149, 187n; "An Ordinary Evening in New Haven," 137, 150, 188n; "The River of Rivers in Connecticut," 129; "The Rock," 31, 137; "Sunday Morning," 136, 147n; "Three Academic Pieces," 187n; *Transport to Summer*, 134

Stone, Robert: *Dog Soldiers*, 17, 59; *A Hall of Mirrors*, 59

A Story-Teller's Story (Sherwood Anderson), 17

Styron, William: *The Long March*, 77n

Sukenick, Ronald: *98.6*, 18

The Sun Also Rises (Ernest Hemingway), 16

Sweeney Agonistes (T. S. Eliot), 16

Tamar and Other Poems (Robinson Jeffers), 16

Tanner, Tony: on *V.*, 72; *City of Words*, 58, 72, 183n

Tate, Allen: as literary influence, 29

Theocritus, 25

Theroux, Paul: *The Family Arsenal*, 17; *The Great Railway Bazaar*, 17

Tiger, Lionel: *The Imperial Animal* (with Robin Fox), 71–72n; *Men in Groups*, 71–72n

The Time of Man (Elizabeth Madox Roberts), 16

Tolstoi, Leo, 154

Toomer, Jean: *Cane*, 16

Toynbee, Arnold: *A Study of History*, 23

transition: A Quarterly Review, 27

Twain, Mark, 133, 160; *The Adventures of Huckleberry Finn*, 65, 69

Tytell, John: *Naked Angels: The Lives and Literature of the Beat Generation*, 66n

Updike, John, 48, 50, 160, 163; "The Blessed Man of Boston...," 183n; *The Centaur*, 77n; *A Month of Sundays*, 17; *Picked-Up Pieces*, 17; *Rabbit, Run*, 48, 50

Valéry, Paul, 11–12n

Vargas Llosa, Mario, 20n

Vendler, Helen, 38, 96, 102; on Frank O'Hara, 94; on Adrienne Rich, 92; on Wallace Stevens, 139

Vidal, Gore: *Burr*, 70; *1876*, 17, 70; *Matters of Fact and Fiction*, 17

Vinal, Harold, 187n

Virgil: *The Eclogues*, 25

Voices: A Quarterly of Poetry, 187n

Vonnegut, Kurt, Jr., 37; *Cat's Cradle*, 59; *Player Piano*, 57; *The Sirens of Titan*, 57

Wakoski, Diane, 39

Walsh, Thomas F.: *Concordance to the Poetry of Wallace Stevens*, 144n, 188n

Warren, Robert Penn: as literary influence, 29; *Or Else*, 79

Waugh, Evelyn, 159n, 187n

Weiss, Theodore, 96

Welty, Eudora, 160; *The Golden Apples*, 64–65, 67; *The Optimist's Daughter*, 77n

West, Nathanael, 62; *Miss Lonelyhearts*, 181n

West, Paul: *Gala*, 18

Wharton, Edith, 62, 160; *A Mother's Recompense*, 16
White Buildings (Hart Crane), 16
Whitman, Walt, 4, 5, 7, 118, 131, 159n; as poetic influence, 84–85; preface to *Leaves of Grass*, 5
Wilder, Thornton, 59
Williams, John A.: *The Man Who Cried I Am*, 60, 183n; *Sissie*, 77n
Williams, William Carlos, 30, 35n, 54, 86, 108n; as poetic influence, 29, 37, 81, 84–85; "Asphodel," 105, 155; *The Desert Music*, 31; *In the American Grain*, 16; *Journey to Love*, 31; *Paterson*, 79; *Spring and All*, 16
Wilson, Edmund, 160
Wilson, William S.: *Why I Don't Write Like Franz Kafka*, 18
Winters, Yvor, 29
Woiwode, Larry: *Beyond the Bedroom Wall*, 18
Wolfe, Tom: *The Electric Kool-Aid Acid Test*, 53n, 192n
Wolfley, Lawrence G.: on *Gravity's Rainbow*, 74n
Woolf, Virginia, 20, 159n
Wordsworth, William: compared to Stevens, 139–140n; preface to *Lyrical Ballads*, 43n; *The Prelude*, 94; "Resolution and Independence," 37
Wright, James, 35, 37, 82; *To a Blossoming Pear Tree*, 18
Wright, Richard, 18, 61, 160, 183–184n; *Black Boy*, 15, 61–62; *Native Son*, 15, 61–62

Yeats, William Butler, 9n, 20, 35n, 133, 144, 159n; as poetic influence, 29

Ziolkowski, Theodore: *Dimensions of the Modern Novel*, 22
Zweig, Paul: on William Dickey, 93; *Three Journeys*, 17, 183n

Compositor: Typesetting Services of California

Text: VIP Bembo
Display: VIP Bembo

www.ingramcontent.com/pod-product-compliance
Lightning Source LLC
Chambersburg PA
CBHW071204240426
43668CB00032B/2078